Also by Roland Mesnier

Dessert University

All the President's Pastries

Roland Mesnier's
BASIC to
BEAUTIFUL
CAKES

ROLAND MESNIER and LAUREN CHATTMAN

Photographs by John Uher

Simon & Schuster

NEW YORK   LONDON   TORONTO   SYDNEY

SIMON & SCHUSTER
Rockefeller Center
1230 Avenue of the Americas
New York, NY 10020

First Simon & Schuster hardcover edition October 2007

SIMON & SCHUSTER and colophon are registered trademarks of Simon & Schuster, Inc.

For information about special discounts for bulk purchases, please contact
Simon & Schuster Special Sales at 1-800-456-6798 or business@simonandschuster.com

Designed by Joel Avirom and Jason Snyder

Manufactured in the United States of America

10 9 8 7 6 5 4 3 2 1

Library of Congress Cataloging-in-Publication Data

Mesnier, Roland.
  [Basic to beautiful cakes]
  Roland Mesnier's basic to beautiful cakes : learn how to make simple,
perfect cakes from the legendary White House pastry chef, and how to
transform them into spectacular showpieces for special occasions / by
Roland Mesnier, with Lauren Chattman.
      p. cm.
  Includes bibliographical references and index.
  ISBN 978-0-7432-8789-0 (alk. paper)
  1. Cake. I. Chattman, Lauren. II. Title. III. Title: Basic to
beautiful cakes.

TX771.M3934 2007
641.8′653--dc22

                              2007027460

ISBN-13: 978-0-7432-8789-0
ISBN-10:   0-7432-8789-4

Dedication

When you make a cake, you truly express your desire to
please the people you love and show them how much you
care. For making the world a warmer and happier place,
I dedicate this book to everyone who has shared his or
her artistry and passion through cake baking.

ACKNOWLEDGMENTS

I would like to thank the following people for their support and encouragement as I worked through the years to develop my cake baking skills at the White House and began a new career as a cookbook author:

My wife, Martha, for her understanding as I spent so many hours in the White House kitchen and on the road, and for typing and proofing the many pages of this book. Also, my son, George, for his support.

My brother, Jean Mesnier, who introduced me to the pastry world. All my other brothers and sisters for their support: Gabriel Mesnier, Lucien Mesnier, Geneviève Guyez, Bernard Mesnier, Serge Mesnier, René Mesnier, and Marie Thérèse Mesnier.

Great thanks to Sydny Miner, a wonderful editor and advisor.

Thanks to Angela Miller, who has guided me in my second career as a cookbook author.

Lauren Chattman, for her work on *Basic to Beautiful Cakes*. May we write many more books together.

John Uher and his staff for the incredibly realized cakes, perfectly photographed. You are artists!

Kathie Ness, once again, for sharp-eyed copy editing.

Michelle Rorke and Laura Holmes in editorial at Simon & Schuster; Jackie Seow, of the Simon & Schuster art department; Elizabeth Hayes in publicity. And a special thanks to Deirdre Muller, who is always a pleasure and a great help.

Many thanks to Ted Conklin and the staff of the American Hotel in Sag Harbor, New York. I'm always inspired when I visit!

Jack Bishop for his practical advice on writing about baking.

First Ladies Rosalynn Carter, Nancy Reagan, Barbara Bush, Hillary Clinton, and Laura Bush, who will always be inspirations to me.

Special thanks to all my colleagues, friends, and supporters: Michel Finel for always sharing ideas; Michel Galand for his friendship and support; Michel and Janet Bus for their hospitality in Sag Harbor.

Many thanks to Yvon Hezard, my great friend and a very talented pastry chef, who gave me a great helping hand in making the cakes for the photo shoot.

Thank you to Mr. Bodo von Alvensleben, former general manager of the Princess Hotel in Bermuda, for encouraging me and making it possible for me to exhibit at the culinary salons in New York City.

I want to also thank the Académie de Cuisine and its owners, François and Patrice Dionot, and the school's wonderful pastry chef, Mark Ramsdel.

Many thanks once again to Brian Maynard and Justin Newby for the donations from KitchenAid.

CONTENTS

INTRODUCTION

I grew up in a rural French town in the 1940s. I was one of nine children; our family didn't have much money. My father worked for the railroad, in the maintenance department. My mother also worked for the railroad: Whenever a train was approaching, a bell would ring in our house; my mother would run out to the tracks that crossed the road where our house stood and close the gates on either side so that the dairy farmers leading their cows across the track from the pasture to the farm for milking four times a day wouldn't be in danger. She did this job seven days a week, from 5:30 in the morning until 9:30 at night, and if she had to leave the house, one of us kids would have to be there to listen for the bell and close the gates.

The house where I grew up had no oven. We bought bread at the village bakery, but we couldn't afford to buy cake there. Maybe three or four times a year on special occasions—a religious confirmation or a brother's return from military service—my mother would make her famous mocha cake, a simple genoise, with rough flour from the local mill and eggs from our own chickens. She baked it on top of the stove in a covered cast-iron pan. Her buttercream had just three ingredients: pure, rich country butter from the farm next door, confectioners' sugar, and coffee, for which she had to scrimp and save. I cannot exaggerate our excitement when she would bring this lopsided but wonderfully fragrant cake to the table. It was her pride to be able to produce, with so few resources, something so delicious. She presented it with much feeling, and was rewarded with our shouts of anticipation and our moans of enjoyment as we savored every bite.

I thought often of those intimate celebratory moments throughout my career, as I tried to create the same excitement and emotion with my desserts, first as a pastry chef in restaurants and hotels throughout Europe and the U.S. and then as White House pastry chef for twenty-five years. Looking back, I have to say that while the spectacular State Dinner desserts I created as tributes to foreign governments were received with admiration, it was the cakes I made to celebrate personal occasions—like birthdays, anniversaries, graduations, and weddings—that elicited the most heartfelt feeling.

At the White House, I made cakes for presidents, their families, and their guests—a disparate group including Chief Justice William Rehnquist, Prime Minister Nakasone of Japan, and Bob Hope. Each cake was designed with the guest of honor in mind. In June of 2006 I was called out of retirement to design a birthday cake for George W. Bush, who was turning sixty. I decorated the cake with sugar pieces representing the important places and moments in his life: the house in Midland, Texas, where he was born; his graduation from Yale; a Texas Rangers cap to represent his purchase of the baseball team; the emblem of Austin, where he was governor; and 1600, the number of acres of his ranch and the address of the White House. My longtime assistant Susie Morrison and I wheeled the cake to his table, and I knew it would be the last one I would make for a president. When he studied it, he had tears in his eyes. I felt it was a job well done.

Cakes, Basic to Beautiful

I may have known only one cake as a child, but in my professional life I pride myself on making a new cake to commemorate each occasion, and to do so with ease. I was so lucky with my job at the White House. Unlike most pastry chefs, who produce the same menu items over and over again, maybe changing a few desserts with the seasons, I had no set menu and no fixed repertoire. My work demanded just the opposite—it called for a never-ending stream of new desserts. It was a challenge, but it was also my favorite part of the job. I was always thinking, always learning.

When I brought a cake to the table, I wanted to surprise people with something that they had never seen before. But it was never purely a matter of changing the appearance of a cake. Over the years, I experimented with and reworked every cake, filling, and frosting recipe I knew, so that I really owned them. I've probably made upside-down cake fifty different ways, and the version I present here takes all of that experience into account.

When I was writing my first book, *Dessert University*, I included just a handful of the hundreds of cakes I made during my time at the White House. They were some of my favorites, but there were many more, so special to me for so many reasons, that wouldn't fit. I knew then that I'd write a book devoted to the subject. In it, I'd not only have room for many more recipes, but I'd be able to reveal the secrets to making new cakes for every occasion. I always felt a little guilty when people wondered at my ability, after so many years, to come up with brand-new cakes, sometimes at a moment's notice. The fact is that I rely on a surprisingly small file of basic, foolproof recipes, perfected over the course of my long career. These foundation recipes allow me to experiment with new flavor and texture combinations and to build new cakes with confidence. Take my genoise recipe, which is not much different from my mother's: I use it for my upside-down cakes because it absorbs the juices from the fruit so beautifully. It forms the layers in the First Ladies' Strawberry Cake, a strawberries-and-whipped-cream extravaganza. When I add some instant espresso powder to the batter, it becomes Coffee Genoise, which can be served as is, covered with Chocolate Mousse, or covered with Mocha Buttercream, depending on the occasion.

But genoise alone cannot sustain a pastry chef's career. A successful cake baker keeps his or her audience and the occasion in mind. Does the guest of honor love moist chocolate cakes? I turn to my Chocolate Soufflé Cake and go from there. Are they allergic to wheat and dairy? Carrot cake made with spelt flour is the place to start. Is the chocolate cake going to be served at a barbecue or a black-tie dinner? Is the carrot cake for a ladies' luncheon or for a family reunion with a lot of kids? The occasion will dictate how a cake is filled, frosted, and decorated.

This book gathers together more than twenty of my favorite basic cakes, the ones I turned to time and again when designing something new. They're loosely organized into the categories that made sense to me as I developed my repertoire: "American"-style cakes that I learned to bake at the White House, like yellow cake, banana cake, and applesauce cake; three very different styles of cheesecake that saw me through countless occasions; cakes with nuts and chocolate, an essential category for any pastry chef; cakes for people with dietary restrictions. At the end of the book I return to my French roots, with recipes for cakes made with puff pastry and pâte à choux.

When I decided to write a book about cakes, I didn't want to make it just another collection of recipes. I wanted to show how a pastry chef thinks, using experience and imagination to spin old desserts into new ones. So in this book, each recipe is really a series of three recipes that increase in complexity. For example, the modest Hazelnut Ring Tea Cake becomes a rich dinner party dessert when glazed with shiny chocolate. It can be transformed further into a grand birthday cake (originally designed for President Reagan) with the addition of whipped cream and some caramelized phyllo as a crowning decoration. By reading through each version of the recipe, you will see how I could serve the same basic cake one day at a Senators' Spouses Tea and then a few weeks later at President Reagan's birthday gala, and collect compliments on both occasions for two very different desserts.

Wherever possible, I describe the inspiration behind a particular recipe. I hope that once you've read about how I used my most reliable recipes to create cakes tailored to the needs of five Presidents and First Ladies, their families, and their guests, you will recognize some that are right for your own occasions, from casual dinners to birthdays, holidays, and even weddings. After you gain confidence with the techniques, you may even want to design your own cakes. Using some of my building blocks and your own creativity, you can certainly come up with a custom cake that's just right for you.

How to Read the Recipes

Since my retirement, I've taught dozens of cooking classes across the country, and I would say that the biggest mistake home cooks make when baking doesn't have anything to do with technique. It is a simple problem of misreading the recipe directions or not reading them at all. People tend to hurry through the beginning of a recipe—the headnote, the ingredients list, and the early reminders to preheat the oven, grease the pans, and set the racks in a certain position in the oven. Everyone wants to rush right to the fun part, where you blend the eggs, sugar, and flour together.

But headnotes often contain tips that will help you avoid mistakes that others (including myself) have made in the past. The ingredients list is the tool you need to organize, and good organization is one key to success. And those early instructions are there for a reason: An unheated oven will slow you down, and you don't want to be searching for the correct pan at the last minute.

So take a few minutes to read the recipe properly, starting at the very beginning, with the title and the yield. Go through the ingredients list with a pencil and paper and make your shopping list, double-checking to see if you really do have pantry items that you "always" have on hand. Then read the instructions through carefully, making sure you understand the sequence and the timing. Is there a component of the cake that needs to be refrigerated for 24 hours? Is there a subrecipe that is printed elsewhere in the book? Know about these things so you're not caught by surprise—and without dessert.

Finally, outline the recipe on paper, jotting down the major steps, to test yourself. If you get confused constructing this short outline, reread the recipe and try again. Most cakes consist of at least two components, and some have many more. Breaking down the recipe before you begin will help you to see the big picture, which is important when undertaking a construction project like a cake.

As you work your way through, consult the recipe often, to remind yourself of the details. Forgetting an ingredient or a small step can spell disaster, as it did for me once when I was a young apprentice, exhausted from working long hours and staying out late at the lively bars in Hamburg. One morning, I was horrified to see that the eggs I had prepared for a giant pot of pastry cream were curdling instantly as I whisked the hot milk into the pot. What on earth was going on? Out of the corner of my eye, I saw the box of cornstarch I had taken out of the pantry but had never measured into my eggs. Without it, the eggs never had a chance. As the chef walked toward me, I stood squarely in front of the pot and hoped he wouldn't ask what I was hiding. Then when he turned away, I threw the whole batch in the garbage, completely humiliated and ashamed. From then on, I made it part of my routine, no matter how simple the recipe, to check and double-check my ingredients and instructions as I proceeded.

Ingredients for Cakes

One of the most compelling reasons to bake your own cakes instead of buying them from a bakery is the control you have over what goes into them. You can choose your favorite brand of chocolate, the vanilla extract you find most fragrant, apples and berries from the local farmers' market. It goes without saying that the best-quality ingredients will produce the best cakes. Buy your eggs, butter, nuts, and flour at a grocery story with a high turnover and store them properly for the freshest flavor. I love the new organic products that are found everywhere, but I'm careful to purchase them from busy markets and not off dusty shelves of a health food store that does a bigger business in vitamins than in vegetables.

Gather all of your ingredients on the counter before you start putting them together. This way, you will know if you are short one egg well before you need to add the eggs to the mixer. If the ingredients list calls for chopped nuts, chop them now, so that you'll be ready with them later. Pay special attention when the recipe calls for room-temperature ingredients, and after you've gathered everything, let these ingredients stand until they really do come to room temperature. If your butter, eggs, and milk are cold, it will be difficult to blend them into a smooth batter. Improperly blended ingredients will result in a heavy, dense cake instead of a light, airy one.

Occasionally a recipe will call for an uncommon item—praline paste or hazelnut flour, for example—which can be mail-ordered or purchased online. But for the most part the ingredients you will need are available at the supermarket, with an occasional trip to the specialty foods store. In fact, it can seem almost miraculous that so many different types of cakes can be conjured from so few basic ingredients. Here is a list of the items that appear over and over again. Individual recipes will give you more information on unusual ingredients.

BUTTER All of the recipes in this book were tested with unsalted butter. It has a purer, fresher taste than salted butter. When a dessert needs salt, it's better to add it separately. Higher-fat European butter is expensive, and I honestly cannot detect a significant difference in cakes baked with it, so I stick with good-quality supermarket butter. Well wrapped, it will keep in the refrigerator for weeks (unwrapped, it might pick up off-odors from the refrigerator). For longer storage, keep it in the freezer. Defrost frozen butter on the countertop for several hours or in the refrigerator overnight. To soften refrigerated butter, let it stand on the counter until pliable— 15 to 20 minutes, depending on how warm your kitchen is. To hasten the softening, cut it into pieces, but don't soften it in the microwave or you'll risk melting it.

CHOCOLATE When it comes to making most chocolate cakes, I use semisweet and bittersweet chocolate instead of unsweetened baking chocolate. I have found through experience and experimentation that unsweetened chocolate can produce a cake with a slightly bitter taste, which some people like but most don't. The choice of semisweet or bittersweet, as well as the brand, is really up to you. Semisweet chocolate has a milder flavor that some people prefer; bittersweet is deeper and more intense. I absolutely love Valrhona chocolate, and at the White House I used it almost exclusively. But this is a matter of opinion, and if you like Callebaut, Lindt, Ghirardelli, or any other high-quality brand for eating, you will also like it in a cake.

Some chocolate cake batters, such as the biscuit macaroon for the Chocolate Dome Cake, are so light that they would deflate if combined with melted chocolate. In these cases, I gently fold in unsweetened cocoa powder for chocolate flavor. Dutch cocoa has been processed so the acids have been neutralized, giving it, in my opinion, a milder and more pleasant taste. It is my personal preference. But if you like non-alkalized cocoa powder, such as Hershey's, that's fine; it will work in any of these recipes. If you are not sure which type you like, use the cocoa powder you like for hot chocolate. Tasting it this way, with just milk and sugar added, will give you a good idea of the character it will lend to cakes.

For mousses, ganaches, and glazes, I stick with semisweet chocolate for its middle-of-the-road flavor. Semisweet chocolate will produce a mousse, ganache, or glaze with a rich, chocolatey flavor that is not overly intense. This was always important when I had to please a roomful of people with different tastes, not to mention political views! Of course, if you know that everyone eating your cake is a dark chocolate fanatic, go ahead and use bittersweet or even extra-bittersweet. It's a matter of knowing your audience.

Occasionally I call for tempered chocolate to be used in cake decorations. Tempering is the process by which chocolate is gently melted so that when it solidifies again it will still be beautifully shiny rather than grainy and gray. For this task, I use couverture chocolate, which contains a relatively high proportion of cocoa solids and cocoa butter, giving it rich flavor and its characteristic shine. Couverture chocolate is the luxurious chocolate made by such upscale manufacturers as Lindt, Valrhona, and Callebaut. You can find 3- or 4-ounce bars of it wrapped in foil and sold for eating out of hand in gourmet shops and candy stores. You can buy it this way, but since tempering requires at least 1 pound of chocolate, it's cheaper to buy couverture chocolate in bulk, either at a specialty foods store or online (see Resources, page 283).

CRÈME FRAÎCHE A heavy cream that has been thickened and given a slightly tangy taste through the addition of a lactic bacteria culture such as buttermilk or lemon juice. It is possible to make crème fraîche at home, but the process can take up to 24 hours and the results are not uniform. I always buy it at the supermarket, for convenience and reliability.

EGGS All of the recipes in this book were tested with U.S. grade large eggs. There is no nutritional or flavor difference between brown and white, so I usually choose whichever is cheaper. I do make sure to buy my eggs at a supermarket with a quick turnover, for the sake of freshness. But the fact is that it takes a very long time, months usually, for refrigerated eggs to go bad. Moreover, older egg whites whip up higher than very fresh ones.

There are several recipes in this book that call for raw egg whites. Although most of the time, any dangerous bacteria reside in the yolks or on the shells, it is best to err on the side of caution: Raw eggs, including whites, should not be used in food to be consumed by children, the elderly, pregnant women, or anyone in poor health or with a compromised immune system, due to the remote chance that the eggs are contaminated with salmonella. For more on egg safety, see page 26.

FLOUR Flour is categorized by its protein content, which gives cakes their structure. You may find it odd that I rarely call for cake flour, which has the smallest amount of protein, for the cake recipes here. In my experience, cake flour is just too soft for most cakes! I use it when I want to produce very tender baked goods—biscuits and sometimes muffins and occasionally very tender cakes. But in general cakes made with cake flour can fall apart when sliced, and can sag under the weight of even the lightest fillings and frostings.

In recent years, I have met more and more people who are allergic to wheat. For them, spelt flour, made from an ancient variety of wheat that rarely causes an allergic reaction, is a godsend. Spelt flour can be substituted for wheat flour in many cakes in this book, including Perfect Yellow Cake (page 31) and Chocolate Dome Cake (page 169). Spelt flour doesn't require as much liquid as wheat flour for hydration, so you'll need more of it if you want to use it in place of wheat flour. Use 25 percent more spelt flour for a similarly balanced recipe.

Occasionally I use hazelnut or almond flour in a cake. Nut flours are not really flours at all, but nuts ground into a fine powder. They contribute flavor, but not structure, to a cake. To bring out the best in nut flour, toast it on a baking sheet in the oven for a few minutes, just as you would toast whole or chopped nuts. Specific recipes will give exact instructions. Nut flours aren't always carried at supermarkets, but they are available online and through the mail from the Baker's Catalogue (see Resources, page 283).

GELATIN Unflavored gelatin gives shape and stability to mousse and Bavarian cake fillings, allowing the cakes to stand at room temperature without collapsing. Since sheet gelatin isn't sold at most supermarkets, I've used powdered gelatin here. The important thing to know when using gelatin is that it requires a two-step soaking process before its thickening properties are activated. First it must be soaked in cool water until it is dissolved. Then it must be heated, either in a warm liquid such as melted chocolate or by itself in a double boiler, to melt it. Once melted, it is ready to work. When stirring warmed gelatin into a room-temperature liquid, make sure to whisk it in quickly and thoroughly. If the melted gelatin is not completely incorporated into the other ingredients before it begins to gel, it will form unappetizing strands.

MILK AND CREAM When a recipe calls for milk, use whole milk or 2-percent milk if you want to shave off a few calories. One-percent and skim milk are too weak and watery to add anything to cake batter.

With some notable exceptions, heavy cream should be well chilled before it is whipped, to achieve the greatest volume. To add a tangy flavor to whipped cream, replace half of it with sour cream or crème fraîche. This combination won't whip up as high as straight whipped cream, and it won't be stiff enough to pipe, but it can be smoothed over a cake or used anywhere that whipped cream is used as a garnish. I like the combination especially on cakes containing fresh fruit.

NUTS Nuts add crunch and rich flavor to many cakes. They can be added to the batter or used decoratively to finish the tops and sides of a frosted cake. Always toast nuts to bring out their flavor and then let them cool completely before using them in or on a cake. The food processor is convenient for chopping nuts finely, but I prefer to do this by hand. Just a few seconds too long in the machine and the nuts will release their oils and become greasy. Store nuts in zipper-lock bags in the freezer, as they turn rancid quickly.

SALT Save your expensive sea salt for the table. The flavor difference between fleur de sel and plain old iodized table salt is indistinguishable in these recipes. Salt enhances the flavors in a cake but plays no chemical role. If you are on a salt-free diet, simply omit the salt.

SUGAR AND OTHER SWEETENERS I use granulated sugar in cake batters. I save confectioners' sugar for glazes, whipped cream, and anything else that requires a quick-dissolving sweetener. When I want to give fruit a quick caramel flavor, I'll cook it briefly in light brown sugar. All of these sugars should be stored in airtight containers to prevent the clumping up and hardening that can occur when sugar comes in contact with moisture in the air.

I keep a bottle of light corn syrup on hand for occasional use in cakes. I use it sometimes in glazes to loosen them without adding too much excess sugar. A small amount of corn syrup in cooked sugar will prevent crystallization.

And I must admit a weakness for artisanal honey; when used in place of sugar in some recipes (Honey Vanilla Sauce, Honey Vanilla Ice Cream), it lends flavor and a velvety texture as well as sweetness.

Equipment

While not tragic, it is certainly aggravating to realize that you need a 10-inch tube pan, not a 10-inch round cake pan, for your Applesauce Cake after you've already mixed your batter. So even before you assemble your ingredients, read each recipe carefully to make sure you have the necessary equipment.

The items listed below will enable you to make and decorate the cakes in this book. It's not a long list, and most of the equipment can be purchased at your local cookware shop or even in the baking aisle of the supermarket. If you have the time and interest, browse around some of the wonderful online baking supply shops (see Resources, page 283), where you will be able to find high-end baking pans, silicone pastry brushes, and professional-quality pastry bags and tips, sometimes at bargain prices. The only big investment I highly recommend is a KitchenAid stand mixer, the most powerful and versatile mixer on the market. I brought one with me to the White House and after nine years I became convinced that it would break down soon, so I bought a second one to have on hand just in case. When I retired sixteen years later, both mixers were running like new. I have one in my own kitchen now, sitting on the countertop and ready to whip egg whites, buttercream, and ganache (if you keep it hidden away, you'll use it less often—these mixers are heavy and a bit inconvenient to take in and out of a cabinet). You can use another type of stand mixer or even a handheld mixer for most jobs, but with the KitchenAid, mixing is not work, but a pleasure.

BAKING PANS Collect the following shapes and sizes as you need them, always buying heavy, sturdy pans that resist warping and denting: one 10-inch round cake pan, two

9-inch round cake pans, two 16 x 12-inch rimmed baking sheets, a 10-cup bundt pan, a 12-cup muffin tin, a 9-inch springform pan, a 10-inch springform pan or 10-inch cake ring, a 9-inch pie plate, and a 9-inch coeur à la crème mold.

BLENDER Essential for making fruit purees and smooth sauces. When I accidentally curdle my vanilla sauce or custard (yes, it even happens to me), I put it in the blender and then strain it and no one knows the difference.

CANDY THERMOMETER Experienced pastry chefs can tell when sugar has reached the proper temperature by feel, but if you are inexperienced, it is best to rely on a candy thermometer for foolproof sugar decorations.

CHEESECLOTH Cheesecloth is necessary for making coeur à la crème and comes in handy for other pastry tasks, such as straining coffee grounds from custards and wrapping loose spices, like whole cloves and star anise, in a bundle so you don't have to fish around in your custard or cream when you want to remove them.

ELECTRIC MIXER An essential piece of equipment for mixing most cake batters and for whipping egg whites and heavy cream. The more you bake, the more money you should invest in a good one that comes with both a whisk and a paddle attachment.

GRATER A Microplane grater is wonderful for finely grating citrus zest. A box grater will work, but it is less efficient and more difficult to clean.

ICE CREAM MACHINE Some of the cakes in this book are made with ice cream; some have ice cream as an accompaniment. You can always use store-bought ice cream, but once you make your own (which is really the same as making vanilla sauce), you will taste the huge difference. For this, you need an ice cream machine. If you are just starting out, buy an inexpensive hand-crank model with a canister that you can chill in the freezer. Once you are committed to making homemade ice cream frequently, you might want to invest in an electric model that chills and stirs the ice cream on the countertop.

KNIVES A sharp chef's knife is essential for chopping nuts and chocolate. A sharp paring knife is essential for fruit. In addition, a top-quality serrated knife makes it a breeze to slice cake layers in half horizontally.

MEASURING SPOONS AND CUPS Success in baking begins with accurate measurement of ingredients. Use clear "liquid" measuring cups for liquid ingredients, "dry" measuring cups for large quantities of dry ingredients, and measuring spoons for small quantities. Level off the dry ingredients so they are flush with the top edge of the cup or spoon. For accurate liquid measurement, judge if you have the proper amount in the cup by checking the lines on the side of the cup at eye level.

MELON BALLERS I have several different sizes, which I use on strawberries, kiwis, and many other fruits as well as melon. I especially like the very smallest, which makes balls about the size of small marbles. It requires very little skill to cut fruit this way for a beautiful and colorful decoration.

MIXING BOWLS These are important not just for mixing cake batter but also for organizing ingredients. Glass bowls can go in the microwave. A stainless-steel bowl set atop simmering water can be used in place of a double boiler.

PAPER DOILIES I use these all the time, in a variety of sizes, as stencils for simple confectioners' sugar and cocoa-powder decorations.

PARCHMENT PAPER A circle of parchment paper at the bottom of a cake pan is insurance that your cake will come out of the pan without incident. Parchment paper (or a Silpat) is also necessary for baking meringue layers and the langue du chat batter I use in some of my cakes. It comes in rolls at the supermarket, but I prefer to stock up on sheets of it, which are available online. Not only are the sheets more economical if you bake a lot (I also use parchment to line baking sheets when I'm making cookies, scones, and bread), but they're just the right size, so there's no waste.

PASTRY BAGS AND TIPS Not only are these items necessary for piping frosting onto a cake, they're also needed for piping pâte à choux and meringue cake layers. Disposable plastic bags are convenient, but coated canvas bags are more economical if you don't mind taking the time to wash them well after every use. There's no need to buy the deluxe set of twenty-five tips. A basic set, including a few plain ones, stars, and a leaf, is all that you will need.

PASTRY BRUSHES Use these to brush syrup on cake layers, to glaze cakes with warm jam, and to brush egg wash on puff pastry and choux puffs to make them shiny. I replace mine frequently, since they collect debris near the handles no matter how well you wash them. Just recently, I've tried the new pastry brushes made with silicone fibers instead of boar bristles or plastic fibers and am delighted at how easily they come clean—as well as the fact that they don't leave unappetizing bristles behind on my cakes.

PLASTIC WRAP Plastic wrap is a baker's best friend, for the way it protects cake layers and assembled cakes in the freezer for months. I also use it to keep cake layers and whole cakes fresh for the short term at room temperature or in the refrigerator.

ROLLING PIN If you are going to make your own puff pastry, you'll need a rolling pin. It's also handy for rolling marzipan before cutting it out. The shape is your choice. I use a straight dowel-style wooden pin because it's what I'm used to and I'm comfortable with it. But other styles—tapered, with handles—work just as well.

SAUCEPANS Good-quality, heavy saucepans are important for making vanilla sauce and pastry cream. Cheaper, lighter pans will scorch these delicate mixtures before they are fully cooked. Saucepans are also necessary for heating cream for ganache, cooking sugar, and as one half of an improvised double boiler for melting gelatin, melting chocolate, and many other cake-related tasks.

SILPAT PAD This silicone pad, the size of a baking sheet, can be used in place of parchment paper when baking meringue cake layers, meringue mushrooms, and langue du chat shapes, and can be used over and over again. It is also necessary for making some of the more advanced sugar decorations in this book, such as the Royal Crown for the Princess Mary Cake.

SPATULAS To scrape cake batter from the sides of a mixing bowl, nothing works like a rubber spatula. Buy the kind made of heatproof plastic or silicone and you will be able to use them to stir cream into boiling caramel without melting them. Offset spatulas, the kind with the thin, flexible metal blade, are used to smooth the top of the cake batter after it is poured into the pan as well as to smooth frostings on the tops and sides of cakes.

STRAINER I use a fine-mesh strainer to strain chunks of fruit from jam as well as to strain lumps from vanilla sauce and pastry cream.

WIRE RACKS Resting your cakes on wire racks before removing them from the pans allows air to circulate underneath them, cooling them quickly so they don't get soggy (or burn the countertop). I also use them, set atop a rimmed sheet pan, for glazing, so that excess glaze can drip down onto the sheet pan without pooling around the cake and creating a mess.

WIRE WHISK A whisk will break up eggs and prevent lumps from forming in your pastry cream. Also use a whisk to make sure that your chocolate is entirely melted and lump-free.

Preparing the Pans

To insure that your cake releases cleanly and easily from the pan, make sure to prepare the pan properly. I suggest greasing flat-bottomed cake pans, lightly dusting them with flour, and then placing a disk of parchment paper on the bottom of the pans for extra security against sticking. For bundt pans, just grease and flour them well to prepare them for the batter.

For greasing, I choose solid vegetable shortening, like Crisco, over butter or cooking spray. Butter is unreliable. Sometimes it will let your cake go, and sometimes it will hold on. With Crisco, your cake is guaranteed to slide right out. The flavor difference is negligible. Avoid cooking spray, which bonds with the flour in the pan to leave an unappetizing, greasy film on the surface of the cake.

If you bake a lot, you might want to place a cup or two of vegetable shortening in the bottom of a tall airtight container, and place a pastry brush dedicated to the purpose of greasing the pans right inside the container. This way, you never have to wash the brush and you don't waste any of the shortening by grabbing a clump of it with a paper towel and then having to discard what you don't use.

Mixing a Cake

Mixing a cake batter is not difficult, but it requires some sensitivity to your ingredients and some knowledge of how they work together to get the best results possible. To ensure success, follow these procedures:

CREAMING BUTTER AND SUGAR The first ingredients mixed together in butter cakes, like the Perfect Yellow Cake, are the butter and sugar. When you do this, you want to combine the ingredients for the smoothest possible batter, but you don't want to whip a lot of air into them, which will cause your cake to rise high in the oven and then fall flat as it cools. The mixer is not a sports car. Resist taking it to its top speed. Instead, beat the sugar and butter on medium or low. As soon as the mixture is nice and creamy, stop. For the quickest and gentlest mixing, make sure your butter is at room temperature.

ADDING LIQUIDS AND FLOUR When it's time to add the milk and eggs, do so a little at a time. Adding too much liquid would be like trying to make yourself drink a full glass of water all at once. You don't want to choke the batter, just quench its thirst. Alternate adding liquid and flour, liquid and flour, always finishing with flour. This way, the last bit of flour will absorb whatever liquid is not yet incorporated into the batter. If you end with the liquid, some of it may stay separate, throwing off the proper balance of ingredients necessary for a successful cake. As insurance, give your batter a quick mix with a rubber spatula, to scrape up any unmixed ingredients at the bottom of the bowl.

WHIPPING EGG WHITES Meringue-based cakes such as a dacquoise and soufflé-type cakes like the Chocolate Soufflé Cake begin with properly whipped egg whites. As I mentioned earlier, older egg whites whip up higher than very fresh ones, but with the proper technique you can achieve sky-high whites from this morning's eggs. To do so, follow this sequence: Whip the whites on high speed until they just hold soft peaks, before you add any sugar. When the whites reach this stage (when you pull the beaters or whisk attachment up from the whites, you will also pull up little points of whipped egg white that will quickly fall over), begin to add the sugar in a slow, steady stream, with the mixer still on high. Only at this point should you begin to add sugar. If you add it earlier, it will dissolve from all the whipping, weighing down your meringue. Furthermore, the intact sugar crystals help to aerate the whites by acting as tiny whips when whirling around.

WHIPPING EGGS AND SUGAR FOR GENOISE BATTER The first step in making a genoise batter is whipping eggs and sugar together over a pot of simmering water. Heating the mixture as it is whipped causes the air bubbles that you are creating to expand greatly, resulting in a light and voluminous mixture. After the mixture reaches a lukewarm temperature, remove it from the heat and beat it on high speed for 5 minutes to increase its volume even more. Then turn the speed to low to break the large air bubbles into tiny ones for the most even rise.

FOLDING If you are making either a genoise or a meringue-based cake, you will have to fold dry ingredients—or in the case of a chocolate cake, melted chocolate—into your egg mixture to finish the batter. The trick is to do so thoroughly without losing any volume. Unless otherwise directed, use this method: Add the ingredients to the bowl. Then use a rubber spatula to scrape up some of the batter or meringue from the bottom of the bowl and turn it over on top of the added ingredients. Turn the bowl slightly, and repeat.

Continue to lift and turn until everything is well combined. Avoid stirring vigorously, or in fact stirring at all, and you won't destroy the air bubbles in the mixture.

TAPPING THE PAN Just in case any large air bubbles or pockets remain in the batter, gently tap the bottom of the pan two or three times on the edge of your countertop. This will burst the bubbles, so your cake will be beautifully even when it comes out of the oven.

Baking a Cake

All of the cakes in this book were tested in my own home oven, a four-year-old electric model made by Maytag. I am blessed with an oven that bakes at a nice even temperature, with no hot spots, so I don't have to rotate the pans as my cake layers bake. If I'm following a reliable recipe, I know my cakes will be done in the recommended time.

Your oven may behave exactly like mine, but it's more likely that it has its own quirks. I highly recommend that you test its temperature with an oven thermometer, which you can buy at any hardware store. You may find that your oven runs 25 to 50 degrees hot or cold, which would explain why your brownies always take 5 minutes longer to bake than they should, or why your chocolate chip cookies are hard as rocks although you bake them for the recommended 10 minutes. Once you have an accurate reading of the temperature in your oven, you can adjust its setting accordingly.

Beyond this, you have to get to know your oven. It may maintain an even baking temperature, or the heating element may cycle on and off during baking, so the oven lurches from a low temperature of, say, 325 to a high of 375. If this is the case, your cake might begin to burn before its interior is cooked through. To combat this possibility, you can try several things: Bake your cake on top of a sheet pan, to insulate it from the extreme heat; tent the top with brown paper, to prevent the crust from burning; or bake the cake on the upper oven rack, farther from the heat source, instead of the middle rack.

If I'm baking two cake layers at once, I prefer to keep them both on the same oven rack, rather than putting one on the top and the other on the bottom. Rotating pans is something that I'm glad to avoid, but if your oven has a hot spot, you have no choice. If one of the cakes is cooking more quickly than the other, let them bake for at least 15 minutes before switching their positions. Earlier than this, and you risk deflating the liquidy batter when you move them.

To check for doneness, insert a toothpick or cake tester into the cake and see if it comes out clean. But don't simply put it vertically through the cake's crust, because as you pull the toothpick out, the rough, hard edges of the crust may wipe away any unbaked batter, giving you a false reading. Instead, use the toothpick to break away a small chunk of the crust before inserting it. Then you will get a better idea of whether or not the cake is baked through.

Cooling a Cake

In general, it is a good idea to let a cake rest in the pan on a wire rack for 5 minutes before turning it over onto a platter or a cardboard cake round. Very hot cakes are more likely to stick to the pan, crack, or break when you invert them. In the case of dense and heavy cakes, such as yellow cake or carrot cake, it's best to leave them in the pan even longer, up to 30 minutes, before turning them over. This amount of time will allow the cake to solidify, so there's less risk of damaging it when unmolding.

Unless otherwise directed, invert cakes directly onto the serving platters or cardboard cake rounds that they will eventually be served from, instead of onto a wire rack. Every time you have to transfer a cake, you run the risk of breaking it, so it's best to transfer it just once, right onto the serving surface.

Assembling and Decorating a Cake

Often, the first step in assembling a cake is slicing it into layers. For the most even layers, use a long, sharp serrated knife. Hold the knife in one hand, against the edge of the cake, while placing your other hand on top of the cake. Use a jigsaw motion to cut into the cake as you rotate it with the other hand, so that you cut into it little by little, all the way around. Keep cutting and rotating until you've cut all the way through. This is the best way to cut even, rather than lopsided, layers.

Some pastry chefs like to apply their soaking syrup with a squeeze bottle, but with this method there is a danger of oversoaking. I prefer to use a pastry brush, which gives me more control. As soon as I've soaked my cake layers, I spread on the filling. In general, fillings should be no more than half the thickness of the cake layer. Otherwise, the richness of the filling will overwhelm the cake. If your cake layer is 1 inch thick, apply no more than ½ inch of buttercream. If you are adding fruit to your filling, then it can be thicker than this, since fruit will lighten the filling.

Buttercream and ganache frostings should be no more than ⅓ inch thick on the top and sides. Any more than this is too heavy and rich. The exception is whipped cream, which has a lighter texture and is lighter on the palate than buttercream or ganache. Half an inch or even more on the top and sides of a cake will not overwhelm it or make it too greasy.

Talent, experience, and ambition will dictate how far you can go with decorations and embellishments. Often the loveliest decorations are the simplest to achieve—grated chocolate pressed into the sides of a cake, fresh raspberries scattered on top and all around a cake, confectioners' sugar sifted over a doily on top of a cake to create a lacy pattern. Making simple flowers and figures with marzipan (see page 274) is the next step. Don't overdo it with these, no matter how much fun you are having molding them. A single rose, perfectly formed, is more beautiful than a cake covered with flowers. Chocolate work is very rewarding. If you learn how to pipe chocolate with a cornet (see page 281), you can use your imagination to draw almost anything in chocolate, like my little chocolate bicyclists for Lance Armstrong's Paris Brest (page 225). Cooked sugar decorations are the most challenging, but if you are an advanced home baker you should attempt them, since they are among the most beautiful and unusual ways to embellish a cake. How far you want to go will depend on the occasion and on how much time and effort you want to spend.

There is one type of decoration that I absolutely detest. When I see a cake covered with fresh flowers, I immediately think it was made by a lazy baker with no imagination. Decorations should add flavor as well as beauty to a cake. There is no guarantee that flowers from the garden, even if they were grown organically and without pesticides, are safe to come in contact with food. Even if the flowers are edible, they will not add anything to the taste of the cake! Use fresh fruit, or nothing at all, rather than decorate with something that you know your guests will have to push aside to get to their dessert.

Refrigerating and Freezing Cakes

Each recipe contains specific recommendations for storing the cakes. In general, cakes that are filled and frosted with buttercream and chocolate freeze beautifully. Well wrapped in plastic, they will stay fresh in the freezer for up to 2 months. Indeed, I have found that there is a better marriage of flavors in a cake that has been frozen than in one that has been put together and served fresh. It is similar, I suppose, to the way a soup or stew gets better over time, because its flavors come together as the dish sits.

Cakes that have sticky or soft frostings shouldn't be wrapped before being refrigerated. They'll be fine in the refrigerator, unwrapped, for up to a day. If you want to freeze a cake that has a soft frosting, freeze it for a couple of hours until the frosting hardens, and then lightly drape it with plastic wrap.

Defrost frozen cakes gradually. Overnight in the refrigerator is best. If you let a cake defrost on the countertop, there is a chance, especially on a hot and humid day, that condensation will form on its surface, ruining the frosting. Add delicate decorations—marzipan, chocolate, fresh fruit—once the cake has defrosted completely.

Cakes filled with pastry cream and cakes covered with whipped cream should not be frozen. Pastry cream and whipped cream undergo chemical changes as they freeze, and when they defrost they more often than not separate, causing the cake to become a gloppy mess. With these cakes, freeze the baked cake layers, defrost them in the refrigerator, and then assemble the cake no more than 1 day in advance.

Serving Your Cake

To be honest, slicing a cake is the job I hate the most, and I always try to pass the task on to someone else if I have the chance! To slice a cake beautifully takes great patience and the right technique. First, be prepared with the proper equipment. Have a tall pot of hot water, a sharp serrated or chef's knife, and a kitchen towel ready. Dip the knife in the hot water, wipe it dry with the towel, and quickly push the knife into the cake. A hot knife will cut more easily than a cold one. Don't drag the knife back up through the slice. Instead, pull it out of the cake as soon as its sharp edge is resting against the platter or cardboard cake round. Then dip the knife into the water, wipe it clean with the towel, and slice again. Wiping is important because if there is frosting clinging to the knife, you might smear it onto the next slice as you cut again. Use the knife as a spatula, inserting the tip underneath the slice, to lift it away from the cake and carefully transfer it to a dessert plate.

Some very soft cakes, such as cheesecake, are best sliced when still frozen. I recommend making cuts in the cake as directed above, wiggling the knife back and forth when it reaches the platter or cake round to create a space between the slices. Leave the slices themselves on the platter or cake round, and let the whole cake defrost. Then when you are ready to serve the dessert, use the knife or a cake server to lift the precut, defrosted slices onto dessert plates.

Very soft and delicate cakes that haven't been frozen can be difficult to slice; the heavy knife sometimes crushes and squeezes the cake so that the neat layers are destroyed. To make slicing easier, freeze soft, freshly baked cakes for 30 minutes just before serving. This time in the freezer will firm them up just enough, without changing their texture, so that they'll slice beautifully.

A Note on Egg Safety

As I travel around the country giving cooking classes and lectures, I am amazed at how many people are panicky about eggs. News reports about salmonella poisoning have sent people running from once-common preparations like meringue frosting, chocolate mousse, and tiramisù. Maybe it's because I grew up in the French countryside and my mother stored our own chickens' eggs in a basket suspended from the ceiling for months at a time, never giving it a second thought when she served us soft-boiled eggs in January that were laid in October, that I have basic faith in the healthfulness and purity of eggs.

As a young pastry chef in Hamburg, London, and Paris, I learned to make many staples of a European pastry chef's repertoire using raw eggs. When I arrived at the White House, I continued to make and serve them. Looking back on my almost fifty years in this profession, I can't think of a single instance when someone became ill from one of my desserts. I took care not to serve anything with raw eggs to young children, pregnant women, or people with compromised immune systems, per the recommendation of the Department of Health. But I never worried. This is not to discount the seriousness of salmonella poisoning. It is only to point out how very remote the chance is that your eggs will carry it.

More worrisome to conscientious pastry chefs is the partial cooking of eggs. Eggs that are heated, but not heated sufficiently, provide a wonderful breeding ground for the bacteria that cause food poisoning. That is why in recipes for Vanilla Sauce, Vanilla Ice Cream, and Pastry Cream, I recommend that you bring the mixture to a bare simmer before removing it from the stove. That way, you will know that it has reached a safe temperature. You can also use an instant-read thermometer, watch for the temperature to register 160 degrees, and stay there for 15 seconds. Have ready a strainer set over a bowl, and moving quickly, strain the mixture the very moment it has reached this point. Whisk it for a few seconds to cool it down, and then whisk for a few seconds every few minutes, so it will cool evenly.

If you've heated these mixtures sufficiently, you don't have to cool them quickly over a bowl of ice, as some food writers recommend. It's not necessary, because no bacteria will have survived the cooking. In fact, a slow cool-down is beneficial, because during this time the mixture continues to cook very gently, resulting in a thicker and richer sauce or cream. When I'm out at a restaurant, I carefully examine any vanilla sauce I'm served before I eat it. An old friend of mine, one of my colleagues at the Savoy Hotel in London, used to say, "If the vanilla sauce runs like water, run away!" Runny sauce hasn't been cooked sufficiently and is not safe to eat, even if it has been cooled over ice and refrigerated immediately.

Many cakes in this book, including the ones filled with pastry cream, taste better when served at room temperature than they do ice-cold from the refrigerator. I have no worries when I leave these cakes out on the counter for a few hours, because I know I've cooked my eggs properly and thus the cakes are not a danger to my guests.

My Favorite American Cakes, Some with Fruit

I became an American citizen shortly after starting work at the White House. Mrs. Carter expedited my application, and I had my new passport two months after I had accepted the job. From the beginning, I was determined to use my European experience to make desserts with an American flair. Because I was often asked to make cakes for special First Family occasions—birthdays, anniversaries, graduation—I felt it was especially important to design cakes that the First Families would connect with emotionally, cakes with familiar flavors and textures with maybe an element of surprise.

In this first section, you'll find recipes typical of this category: Perfect Yellow Cake, Upside-Down Cake, Banana Bundt Cake, and Applesauce Cake, all of which I discovered when I came to America. But these cakes are also very much a product of my history, which includes my apprenticeship in Hamburg and my early career in London and Paris. The brioche "peaches" that embellish the Peach and Spice Upside-Down Cake are similar to pastries I made in France as a young pastry cook, and the marzipan ladybug decoration is something I learned in Germany many years ago. The Applesauce Cake soaked in a cranberry syrup is something I devised with a classic Rum Baba in mind. Even the First Ladies' Strawberry Cake, which showcases Americans' favorite fruit, is made with a European-style genoise, instead of the yellow cake or pound cake most American home bakers use.

1. PERFECT YELLOW CAKE

I use this batter to make everything from cupcakes to wedding cakes. It was the building block of two White House wedding cakes—one for President George H.W. Bush's daughter and one for Mrs. Clinton's brother. Thus tested at Camp David and in the Rose Garden, it is ready to serve your basic and not-so-basic cake needs.

PERFECT YELLOW CAKE FILLED with RASPBERRY JAM

Serves 8

FOR THE CAKE:

3 cups cake flour (not self-rising)

2 teaspoons baking powder

¼ teaspoon salt

12 tablespoons (1½ sticks) unsalted butter, softened

1 cup plus 3 tablespoons granulated sugar

2 large eggs

2 large egg yolks

1 cup milk

1 tablespoon pure vanilla extract

½ tablespoon grated lemon zest

TO FINISH:

⅔ cup raspberry jam

2 tablespoons confectioners' sugar

This version of Perfect Yellow Cake, unfrosted and filled with jam, was casual enough to serve at the many pool parties thrown by the Bush family kids during the summers that George H. W. Bush was in the White House. Horseshoes, water polo, and just plain splashing around were the afternoon activities. The menu was usually hot dogs, burgers, watermelon, lemonade, and this cake.

1. Preheat the oven to 375 degrees. Grease and flour a 10-inch round cake pan with 3-inch-high sides.

2. Sift the flour, baking powder, and salt together in a medium bowl. Set aside.

3. Combine the butter and sugar in the bowl of an electric mixer fitted with the paddle attachment. Beat on medium-low speed until well combined but not fluffy. And the eggs and egg yolks and beat until well combined, scraping down the bowl once or twice as necessary.

4. With the mixer on low speed, add half of the flour mixture and stir until just combined. Add half of the milk and stir until just combined. Repeat with the remaining flour and milk. Stir in the vanilla and lemon zest.

5. Scrape the batter into the prepared pan and smooth the top with a spatula. Bake until a toothpick inserted into the center comes out clean, about 40 to 45 minutes.

6. Let the cake sit in the pan on a wire rack for 5 minutes. Then run a sharp paring knife around the edge to loosen the cake, invert the pan over another wire rack, and unmold the cake. Reinvert it onto another wire rack so it is right side up. Let it cool completely.

7. To finish: Use a sharp serrated knife to split the cake into two horizontal layers. Place the bottom layer on a serving platter. Spread the jam evenly over the cake. Top with the remaining cake layer. Sift the confectioners' sugar evenly over the top of the cake. Slice it into eight wedges, and serve.

YELLOW CAKE ICE CREAM SUNDAES

Serves 10

1 Perfect Yellow Cake (page 32), cooled to room temperature

²/₃ cup raspberry jam

1 recipe Light Chocolate Sauce (page 260)

2 pints Vanilla Ice Cream (page 252) or store-bought vanilla ice cream

Slices of jam-filled Perfect Yellow Cake dressed up with vanilla ice cream and chocolate syrup are a fun way to celebrate a birthday. The classic combination of vanilla, chocolate, and raspberry is sure to please young and old. Who doesn't like to eat his own cake-based sundae? Depending on how ambitious you are, you can make your own ice cream or use your favorite store-bought brand. Do make the Light Chocolate Sauce yourself, though—it's so easy and a thousand times better than the kind that comes in a squirt bottle.

1. Use a sharp serrated knife to split the cake into two horizontal layers. Place the bottom layer on a serving platter. Spread the jam evenly over the cake. Top with the remaining cake layer.

2. Cut the cake into ten wedges. Place each wedge on a dessert place. Pour some of the chocolate sauce over each wedge so that it drips down the sides of the cake but does not completely cover the slice. Top each slice with a small scoop of ice cream.

CHERRY ALMOND TRIFLE CAKE

Serves 10

1 Perfect Yellow Cake (page 32), cooled to room temperature

1 cup sour cherry jam

$1/2$ cup Amaretto or other almond-flavored liqueur

2 tablespoons cold water

$1/2$ envelope unflavored gelatin

2 cups Pastry Cream (page 249)

1 cup heavy cream, chilled

Two 14-ounce cans pitted sweet black cherries, drained and patted dry

1 recipe Sweetened Whipped Cream (page 248)

One of my favorite pastry tricks from my White House years is assembling the ingredients for a classic trifle back in the cake pan, rather than in a large glass bowl. The flavor and texture are the same as a classic trifle, but the presentation is more formal and glamorous. Because it can be made well ahead of time (I used to make it 2 weeks in advance and freeze it), I often made it for large White House receptions during the holidays, when I had to prepare large tables of desserts, including cookies, candies, and Bûche de Noël. Whenever I didn't make it, people who had been at the parties in years past would ask where it was.

1. Using a sharp serrated knife, slice the cake into five equal layers, each about $1/4$ inch thick. Place the bottom layer in a clean 10-inch cake pan with 3-inch sides.

2. Spread $1/3$ cup of the jam over each of three of the remaining cake layers. Stack the four remaining layers, placing the three jam-covered layers on the bottom so that the jam holds the cake together.

3. Slice this jam-filled layer cake in half, and then cut three $1/4$-inch-thick strips from the straight edge of one of the halves. Arrange the strips around the edges of the cake-lined pan, forming a border around the perimeter. Trim away and discard any excess.

(cont. on next page)

4. Slice the remaining jam-filled cake into 1-inch cubes. Place the cubes in a bowl and sprinkle with half of the Amaretto, stirring several times to make sure that all the cubes have been moistened.

5. Place the water in a small heatproof bowl and sprinkle the gelatin on top. Let stand until softened, 1 to 2 minutes. Then place the bowl over a small saucepan of barely simmering water and whisk constantly until the gelatin is completely dissolved. Quickly whisk the gelatin mixture into the Pastry Cream. Whisk the remaining Amaretto into the pastry cream mixture.

6. Whip the cream with an electric mixer until it holds soft peaks. Fold the whipped cream into the pastry cream mixture.

7. Reserve about 12 cherries for garnish. Arrange some of the genoise cubes in a single layer across the bottom of the cake-lined pan. Spoon some of the cream mixture over the cubes and smooth with a spatula. Arrange a layer of cherries on top of the cream mixture. Continue to build the layers, finishing with a layer of cream. Cover with plastic wrap and refrigerate overnight or for up to 2 days.

8. To serve: Invert the cake onto a cutting board and then reinvert onto a serving platter. Decorate with the reserved cherries and Sweetened Whipped Cream rosettes (see page 273), and serve.

2. UPSIDE-DOWN CAKES, SIMPLE TO SPECTACULAR

During my twenty-five years at the White House, I never tired of making upside-down cakes, and the First Families never tired of eating them. They're simple, colorful, and delicious. There is a version for every occasion: Blueberry Upside-Down Cake with a yogurt sauce is a light breakfast cake; I often served Cherry Upside-Down Cake with a Lattice of Whipped Cream at White House teas or for family dinners. The peach version is a beautiful special-occasion dessert. The brioche "peaches" that serve as a garnish give off an intoxicating scent as they bake. On the days when I would bake them, the Secret Service agents posted on the roof of the White House near the vent from the pastry shop would call down to tell me that I was driving them crazy!

Most people are familiar with pineapple upside-down cake, made with canned pineapple rings. My cakes are a little bit different. I don't like to caramelize the fruit with brown sugar because I think that technique makes the cake too sweet. Another change from most recipes: My versions have more fruit, about equal amounts of fruit and cake batter. This abundance makes for a particularly moist and fresh-tasting cake. Be sure to line your pan with parchment before adding the fruit. Then you can stop worrying that the fruit will stick to the pan when you attempt to invert it onto a serving platter.

BLUEBERRY UPSIDE-DOWN CAKE with YOGURT SAUCE

Serves 10

3 cups fresh blueberries

4 large eggs

½ cup sugar

¾ cup plus 1½ tablespoons all-purpose flour

Pinch salt

1 teaspoon pure vanilla extract

¼ cup red currant or grape jelly

2 cups plain yogurt, mixed with ¼ cup honey or ½ cup fruit preserves of your choice; or 2 cups fruit yogurt, stirred

Wholesome, healthy ingredients like blueberries and yogurt make this cake a good choice for breakfast or brunch. I found myself making it more often when I discovered delicious Greek yogurt, which makes absolutely the best garnish. In place of plain yogurt, you can serve fruit-flavored yogurts in contrasting colors. Little dollops of peach, raspberry, and lemon yogurt placed alongside slices of cake make a pretty presentation.

1. Preheat the oven to 375 degrees. Rinse the blueberries under cold water and transfer them to a plate lined with paper towels to air-dry. Pick through them and remove any stems.

2. Grease a 9 x 2-inch-deep round cake pan. Line the bottom of the pan with parchment paper, and grease the paper. Dust the pan with flour, and tap out any excess. Arrange the blueberries in an even layer on the bottom of the pan.

3. Pour 2 inches of water into a medium saucepan, and bring to a bare simmer. Combine the eggs and sugar in the bowl of an electric mixer fitted with the whisk attachment. Place the bowl over the simmering water and whisk constantly, by hand or with a handheld mixer, until the egg mixture is just lukewarm to the touch, 86 to 90 degrees on an instant-read thermometer.

4. Return the bowl to the mixer and whisk on high speed for 5 minutes. Then reduce the speed to medium and whisk until the mixture is completely cool, thick, and shiny, another 12 minutes.

5. Using a rubber spatula, fold in the flour, salt, and vanilla. Pour the batter over the blueberries. Tap the cake pan on the counter four or five times to eliminate any large air bubbles. Bake until a toothpick inserted into the center comes out clean, about 40 minutes.

6. Remove the pan from the oven and let the cake cool in the pan for 5 to 10 minutes. Turn the cake out onto a cardboard cake round, berry side up. Carefully peel away the parchment. Place the round on a wire rack and allow the cake to cool completely.

7. Heat the jelly in a small pot until it is loose and just warm. Pour the jelly through a fine-mesh strainer into a small bowl. Using a pastry brush, brush the warm jelly over the blueberries to glaze them. Slice, and serve with the yogurt sauce on the side. Blueberry Upside-Down Cake is best served on the day it is baked. (Alternatively, leave the parchment paper on top of the cake as it cools. When it is completely cooled, wrap it in plastic wrap and freeze it for up to 2 weeks. Remove the paper, glaze the berries, and slice it while it is still slightly frozen, for beautiful, clean slices.)

CHERRY UPSIDE-DOWN CAKE
with a LATTICE of WHIPPED CREAM

Serves 10

FOR THE CAKE:

Three 15-ounce cans pitted cherries, preferably black Oregon cherries, rinsed and patted dry with paper towels

4 large eggs

1/2 cup granulated sugar

3/4 cup plus 1 1/2 tablespoons all-purpose flour

Pinch salt

1 teaspoon pure vanilla extract

4 tablespoons unsalted butter, melted and cooled

1/4 cup red currant or grape jelly

FOR THE LATTICE:

2 cups heavy cream

3 tablespoons confectioners' sugar

1 teaspoon pure vanilla extract

1 1/2 cups grated semisweet chocolate

In this version, the genoise batter is enriched with a few tablespoons of butter, making the cake a true dessert. With its lattice of whipped cream, it is beautiful but still casual. I made it for White House family get-togethers, not official functions. Canned cherries are much better than fresh cherries in this cake, because they won't release as much liquid. Look for black Oregon cherries; they're the sweetest. Three cans might seem like a lot of fruit, but that's what this cake is all about.

1. Preheat the oven to 375 degrees. Grease a 9 x 2-inch-deep round cake pan. Line the bottom of the pan with parchment paper, and grease the paper. Dust the pan with flour, and tap out any excess. Arrange the cherries evenly over the bottom of the pan.

2. Pour 2 inches of water into a medium saucepan, and bring to a bare simmer. Combine the eggs and sugar in the bowl of an electric mixer fitted with the whisk attachment. Place the bowl over the simmering water and whisk constantly, by hand or with a handheld mixer, until the egg mixture is just lukewarm to the touch, 86 to 90 degrees on an instant-read thermometer.

3. Return the bowl to the mixer and whisk on high speed for 5 minutes. Then reduce the speed to medium and whisk until the mixture is completely cool, thick, and shiny, another 12 minutes.

FOR SERVING:

Vanilla Ice Cream (page 252) or store-bought vanilla ice cream (optional)

4. Using a rubber spatula, fold in the flour, salt, and vanilla. Spoon about 1 cup of the batter into a small mixing bowl and stir in the butter; then carefully fold the batter-and-butter mixture back into the larger bowl of batter.

5. Pour the batter over the cherries. Tap the cake pan on the counter four or five times to eliminate any large air bubbles. Bake until a toothpick inserted into the center comes out clean, about 40 minutes.

6. Remove the pan from the oven, and let the cake cool in the pan for 5 to 10 minutes. Turn the cake out onto a cardboard cake round, cherry side up. Place the round on a wire rack and allow the cake to cool completely.

7. Heat the jelly in a small pot until it is loose and just warm. Using a pastry brush, brush the jelly over the cherries to glaze them.

8. Place the cream in the bowl of an electric mixer fitted with the whisk attachment, and whip on high speed until soft peaks appear. Add the confectioners' sugar and vanilla, and continue to whip until the cream just holds stiff peaks. Do not overwhip. Spoon some of the cream into a pastry bag fitted with a #4 or #5 star tip, and pipe the whipped cream in a lattice design on top of the cake (see page 273). Use a small spoon to sprinkle the grated chocolate into the openings in the latticework. Serve immediately, or let stand at room temperature for 4 hours before serving—with vanilla ice cream, if desired.

PEACH and SPICE UPSIDE-DOWN CAKE with BRIOCHE "PEACHES"

Serves 10

¼ cup chopped raisins

2 tablespoons plus 1 teaspoon finely chopped candied orange peel

½ teaspoon grated lemon zest

½ teaspoon grated orange zest

6 tablespoons plus ¾ cup cake flour

1 teaspoon baking powder

½ teaspoon baking soda

1 teaspoon ground cinnamon

1 teaspoon ground ginger

½ teaspoon ground cloves

½ teaspoon ground allspice

Pinch ground nutmeg

8 tablespoons (1 stick) unsalted butter, softened

5 tablespoons granulated sugar

5 tablespoons plus ½ cup packed light brown sugar

2 large eggs, at room temperature

On its own, this spiced upside-down cake is rustic and homey. Add the brioche "peaches" as a decoration and it becomes a State Dinner–worthy dessert. In fact, during the Clinton administration it was served at a dinner for Prime Minister Tony Blair and Chancellor Helmut Kohl.

1. Preheat the oven to 375 degrees. Grease one 9-inch round cake pan and line it with parchment paper.

2. Stir the raisins, candied orange peel, lemon zest, orange zest, and 1 teaspoon of the cake flour together in a medium bowl. Set aside.

3. Sift the remaining ¾ cup plus 1 tablespoon and 2 teaspoons cake flour with the baking powder, baking soda, cinnamon, ginger, cloves, allspice, and nutmeg into a medium bowl.

4. Combine 5 tablespoons of the butter, the granulated sugar, and the 5 tablespoons brown sugar in the bowl of an electric mixer fitted with the paddle attachment. Beat on medium-high speed until smooth. Do not overbeat. Add the eggs and then the yolk, one at a time, scraping down the sides of the bowl after each addition.

5. Add one fourth of the flour mixture to the bowl and mix to combine. Then add 2 tablespoons of the buttermilk and mix to combine. Repeat, ending with the flour mixture, mixing until smooth and scraping down the sides of the bowl after each addition. Stir in the raisin mixture.

1 large egg yolk, at room temperature

6 tablespoons buttermilk, at room temperature

8 large ripe peaches, peeled, halved, pitted, and halved again

1 recipe Vanilla Sauce (page 251)

Brioche "Peaches" (recipe follows)

6. Spread the remaining 3 tablespoons butter over the bottom of the parchment-lined pan. Sprinkle the remaining ½ cup brown sugar over the butter. Place the peaches on top of the brown sugar, arranging them on their sides, tight together, in concentric circles, starting at the edge and going toward the center. Pour the cake batter over the peaches and smooth it with a spatula. Bake until a toothpick inserted into the center of the cake comes out clean, 30 to 40 minutes.

7. Run a sharp knife around the edge of the pan and invert the cake onto a serving plate. Carefully peel away the parchment paper. Serve warm, or let stand at room temperature for up to 8 hours before serving.

8. Just before serving, pour the Vanilla Sauce around the cake. Place one brioche "peach" on top of the cake and arrange the others around the cake, on top of the sauce.

Brioche "Peaches"

Makes 10 small pastries

1½ teaspoons salt

5 tablespoons plus 1½ cups sugar

6 tablespoons warm water

3 cups all-purpose flour

1 ounce fresh yeast, or 1⅓ envelopes active dry yeast

5 large eggs

1 cup (2 sticks) unsalted butter, softened

2½ cups Pastry Cream (page 249)

2 cups apricot jam

Red food coloring

10 green marzipan stems (page 275)

10 green marzipan leaves (page 275)

10 marzipan ladybugs (page 275; optional)

These balls of brioche filled with Pastry Cream look like beautiful blushing peaches. They make a stunning accompaniment to Peach and Spice Upside-Down Cake, or they can be served on their own as individual desserts, with a little Vanilla Sauce on the side if you like. Flavor the Pastry Cream with 2 tablespoons of Grand Marnier, rum, or any other liqueur of your choice if you like.

1. Combine the salt, the 5 tablespoons sugar, and 2 tablespoons of the warm water in the bowl of an electric mixer fitted with the dough hook. Stir on low speed to dissolve the salt and sugar. Add the flour and stir to combine.

2. Combine the remaining 4 tablespoons warm water and the yeast in a small bowl and let stand until the yeast dissolves and the mixture becomes foamy.

3. With the mixer on medium speed, add 4 of the eggs, one at a time. Continue to stir for 5 to 7 minutes, until the dough is smooth and very firm.

4. With the mixer still on medium, slowly add the remaining egg and then the yeast mixture to the dough. Mix on low speed until the dough is silky and elastic and detaches from the sides of the bowl, about 15 minutes.

5. With the mixer still on low, add the butter, 4 tablespoons at a time, making sure that it is incorporated before adding more. The addition of all the butter should take about 3 to 4 minutes. When it is all incorporated, the dough should be glossy and elastic.

6. Cover the bowl with a clean kitchen towel and let it stand in a warm (about 80 to 85 degrees), draft-free place until it has doubled in size, about 1½ hours.

7. Deflate the dough by flipping it over in the bowl five or six times. Cover it again with the towel, place it in the refrigerator, and leave it overnight or no longer than 24 hours.

8. Line a baking sheet with parchment paper. Divide the dough into twenty equal pieces, each the size of a large marble. Place the dough balls on the baking sheet, spacing them 2 inches apart. Flour your hand, and press each ball with your palm to flatten it about halfway. Lightly drape the flattened balls with plastic wrap and let stand in a warm (about 80 to 85 degrees), draft-free place until they have doubled in size, about 45 minutes.

9. Preheat the oven to 425 degrees. Bake the brioche balls until they are golden and risen, 12 to 15 minutes. Let them cool completely on the baking sheet. Then place the baking sheet in the freezer to chill the balls, about 45 minutes (you don't want to freeze them completely).

10. Remove the baking sheet from the freezer. Use a melon baller to break through the surface of the pastry and make a cavity for the Pastry Cream.

11. Fit a pastry bag with a #4 tip and fill it with the Pastry Cream. Insert the tip in the hole made with the melon baller. Fill with Pastry Cream, so that a little bit of the cream is coming out of the hole. Repeat with the remaining brioche balls. Attach two balls to each other, using the Pastry Cream as glue, so they look like a fat peach. Wipe any excess Pastry Cream away with your finger. Repeat with the remaining balls.

12. Place the remaining 1½ cups sugar in a shallow bowl.

13. Bring the apricot jam to a boil in a saucepan, and then push it through a fine-mesh strainer into a bowl. Transfer ¼ cup of the hot jam to a small bowl and stir in a drop of red food coloring.

14. Using a pastry brush cover each "peach" all over with the plain apricot jam. Then use another brush to brush the two cheeks of the "peach" with the colored jam. Roll each "peach" immediately in the granulated sugar. Attach a marzipan stem and leaf to the stem end of each "peach," pushing them into the brioche so they stay. Dab a little bit of jam on the underside of each marzipan ladybug and attach one to each leaf, if desired. Serve immediately or let stand at room temperature for several hours before serving.

Brioche Pizza

I've come up with many simple ways to combine brioche and fruit, since I love them together. Brioche Pizza is one of the easiest and most fun, and you can make it with some leftover brioche dough and Pastry Cream if you've already made brioche peaches:

Take a ball of brioche dough about the size of half a grapefruit, and roll it out on a lightly floured countertop. Flatten it with your hands, leaving a puffy rim, just like pizza dough. Place it on a lightly greased baking sheet and spread about 1 cup of Pastry Cream over the surface. Dot the Pastry Cream with some fresh fruit—peach slices, raspberries, blueberries, whatever you like. Let it rise at room temperature for 45 minutes, and then bake in a 425-degree oven for 35 minutes.

3. BANANA CAKE, THREE WAYS

Don't confuse this cake with banana bread, which is often unpleasantly dense and soggy. This is a real cake, moist but light, with an intense banana flavor. Use very ripe, but not brown, bananas. The recipe is very simple. Even if you've never baked a cake before, with this one you will not fail. Another selling point: This moist, long-keeping cake travels well. Bring it along when you visit Grandma, your college freshman, or any good friend who appreciates bananas. It will stay fresh in the refrigerator for at least a week and can be frozen for up to 3 months.

BANANA BUNDT CAKE

Serves 12

FOR THE CAKE:

6 medium-size, very ripe (but not overripe) bananas

1 cup all-purpose flour

1 teaspoon baking soda

$\frac{1}{2}$ teaspoon salt

1 teaspoon ground cinnamon

$\frac{1}{2}$ teaspoon ground nutmeg

2 large eggs

1 cup sugar

$\frac{1}{2}$ cup canola or corn oil

TO FINISH:

$\frac{1}{4}$ cup confectioners' sugar

In its simplest form, this is a not-too-sweet breakfast, brunch, or tea cake. A pretty bundt pan will mold the cake into a decorative shape. Just dust it with confectioners' sugar before serving.

1. Preheat the oven to 375 degrees. Grease a 10-cup bundt pan and dust it with flour; tap out any excess.

2. Puree the bananas in a blender or food processor. Measure out 1 cup, reserving any extra for another purpose.

3. Sift the flour, baking soda, salt, cinnamon, and nutmeg together in a medium bowl.

4. Place the eggs, sugar, and oil in a large mixing bowl and beat with an electric mixer on medium-high speed for 5 minutes. Mix in the banana puree until smooth. Add the flour mixture and mix well, scraping down the sides of the bowl once or twice as necessary.

5. Scrape the batter into the prepared pan, and smooth it with a spatula; the batter should come about halfway up the sides of the pan. Bake until a toothpick inserted into the center comes out clean, about 35 minutes.

6. Remove the pan from the oven and immediately invert it onto a wire rack. Unmold the cake and allow it to cool completely. Covered with a cake dome, Banana Bundt Cake will keep at room temperature for up to 3 days, or in the refrigerator for 1 week. Wrapped in plastic wrap and then in aluminum foil, it can be frozen for up to 3 months.

7. Dust the cake with the confectioners' sugar before serving.

BANANA BUNDT CAKE COVERED with CREAM CHEESE FROSTING and GRATED CHOCOLATE

Serves 12

8 ounces Philadelphia brand cream cheese, softened

1/2 cup plus 2 tablespoons confectioners' sugar

1/2 teaspoon pure vanilla extract

1 Banana Bundt Cake (page 48), cooled but not dusted with confectioners' sugar

1 1/2 cups grated bittersweet or semisweet chocolate

With very little effort you can change a simple banana tea cake into a splendid dessert. First, cover it with tangy cream cheese frosting. Then cover the frosting with dark chocolate shavings. A dusting of confectioners' sugar completes the transformation. The velvety cake, smooth frosting, and crunchy chocolate are a perfect study in contrasts. I often made this cake for afternoon teas at the White House, always hosted by the First Lady. It didn't matter what group was visiting—teachers from California, businesspeople from New York, Democratic women from Georgia, Republican women from Texas—there was never a slice left over.

Grate the chocolate on the large holes of a box grater, working quickly so it doesn't soften from the heat of your hands.

1. Combine the cream cheese, the 1/2 cup confectioners' sugar, and the vanilla in the bowl of an electric mixer fitted with the paddle attachment, and mix until smooth.

2. Place the cake on a serving platter. Use a small offset spatula to cover the cake with the cream cheese frosting. Press the grated chocolate into the frosting. Sift the remaining 2 tablespoons confectioners' sugar over the cake, and serve.

EXOTIC BANANA CAKE

Serves 12

1 Banana Bundt Cake
(page 48)

1 small fresh pineapple,
preferably a golden pineapple
from Costa Rica, peeled,
cored, and cut into thin slices

1 large ripe mango, peeled,
pitted, and cut into thin
slices

1 small ripe papaya, peeled,
seeded, and cut into thin
slices

1 navel orange, peeled and
segmented, with as much
pith removed as possible

2 kiwis, peeled and thinly
sliced

1 recipe Mango Sauce (page
264)

In this version, I take the banana cake back to its tropical origins, garnishing it with sliced fresh pineapple, mango, and papaya, and serving it with Mango Sauce. Its fruit flavors are very good in the summertime, especially after a big, spicy meal. Decorating the cake is a lot of fun, because you can use your artistic sense to arrange the fruit in the way that pleases you most.

Place the cake on a serving platter. Arrange the fruit around and on top of the cake. Serve immediately, with the Mango Sauce on the side.

Slicing Pineapples, Mangos, Papayas, and Kiwis

Sometimes fresh fruit makes the most beautiful cake decoration, as with Exotic Banana Cake. But if you've never peeled a whole pineapple, mango, or papaya, you may be confused about where to start. Here are simple directions for preparing the fruits.

Pineapple: Place the pineapple on a cutting board and cut a slice off the top, removing the leaves and rind. Stick a fork in the core so you have something to hold on to, and pare away the rind in thin vertical strips, taking care not to lose too much flesh. Slice off the end. Cut the pineapple in half crosswise, and then remove the woody core by making a V-shaped cut around the center of each half. Then slice the fruit into thin V shapes. To cut the pineapple into rings, cut the peeled pineapple into 1/2-inch-thick slices and then remove the core from each slice with a small biscuit cutter.

Mango: Peel the skin off with a sharp paring knife. Cut the two large oval pieces of flesh away from the hard, fibrous pit in the center. Cut away as much of the remaining flesh as possible, leaving behind any prickly fibers extending from the pit. Once the flesh is cut away from the pit, it can be sliced into cubes, half-moons, or ribbons that can be formed into decorative rosettes.

Papaya: Peel the papaya with a vegetable peeler or a sharp paring knife. Cut it in half lengthwise. Scoop out the seeds with a spoon and discard them. Place each half, cut side down, on the cutting board and cut each one into 4 lengthwise slices. Then cut each piece into thin slices.

Kiwi: Trim off both ends of the kiwi. Place one end on the cutting board and remove the skin in vertical slices with a sharp paring knife. Then turn the peeled kiwi on its side and cut it into thin rounds.

Peach and Spice Upside-Down Cake with Brioche "Peaches"

Aurora Pacifica,
Jacques Cousteau–Style

Princess Mary Cake with Royal Crown
and Madeira Sabayon

Moonwalk Cake

Chocolate Artist's Coeur à la Crème

**Applesauce Cake with
Poached Pears and Pastry Leaves**

Banana Bundt Cake Covered with
Cream Cheese Frosting and Chocolate Shavings

4. AUTUMN APPLESAUCE CAKE

As pastry chef for a quarter of a century at the White House, I was always inspired and excited by the change of seasons. In the fall, when the leaves started to turn color and the sunshine had a mellow, golden cast to it, I'd want to fix warm and cozy desserts for the First Family, desserts with the flavors and colors of autumn. This moist cake is a great base for several great autumn desserts. I like that it is a typical American recipe. Cakes made with applesauce have a long tradition in this country, but they were new to me when I arrived here. I was intrigued by the sometime addition of pineapple, nuts, and maraschino cherries. It sounded like a recipe from the label on a can, but when I tried it I was really pleased with the great texture, with the crunchy nuts and toothsome cherries, the whole thing made moist by the applesauce and pineapple. It became a favorite as I figured out a variety of interesting ways to use it.

WARM APPLESAUCE CAKE with CRANBERRY SYRUP

Serves 12

FOR THE CAKE:

1 cup plus 3 tablespoons all-purpose flour

1 teaspoon baking soda

¼ teaspoon salt

1 teaspoon ground cinnamon

¼ teaspoon ground nutmeg

10 tablespoons (1¼ sticks) unsalted butter, softened

½ cup plus 2 tablespoons sugar

2 large eggs

½ cup applesauce

½ cup raisins

½ cup chopped pecans

½ cup canned crushed pineapple, drained

One 10-ounce jar whole maraschino cherries (about 22 cherries), drained, patted dry, and stemmed

I serve this incredibly fragrant cake at my own Thanksgiving dinner. It's not difficult to make, but the technique may be unfamiliar. After you bake the cake, you keep it in the pan and slowly drizzle the syrup on top of it, so the cake absorbs it like a sponge. Then you keep it warm in the oven until serving. It's unusual, and yet comfortingly familiar with the flavor of apples and cranberries.

1. Preheat the oven to 375 degrees. Grease and flour a 10-inch tube pan.

2. Sift the flour, baking soda, salt, cinnamon, and nutmeg together into a medium bowl.

3. In the bowl of an electric mixer fitted with the paddle attachment, cream together the butter and sugar until smooth. Beat in 1 egg and half of the applesauce. Stir in half of the flour mixture. Beat in the remaining egg and applesauce. Stir in the remaining flour mixture. Stir in the raisins, pecans, and pineapple.

4. Pour the batter into the prepared pan and smooth it with a spatula. Arrange the cherries on top of the batter (they will sink into the batter as the cake bakes). Bake until a toothpick inserted into the center of the cake comes out clean, 35 to 40 minutes. Cool the cake in the pan on a wire rack.

5. While the cake is cooling, make the syrup: Combine the cranberries, 4 cups of the water, and the sugar in a

**FOR THE CRANBERRY
SYRUP**:

One 12-ounce bag fresh or
frozen cranberries

4½ cups water

1½ cups plus 2 tablespoons
sugar

¼ cup fresh lemon juice

2 cups Light Syrup (page 264)

FOR SERVING:

Sweetened Whipped Cream
(page 248)

medium saucepan and bring to a boil. Turn the heat down
to medium-high and cook, stirring occasionally, until the
berries stop popping and are very soft and falling apart,
about 10 to 15 minutes.

6. Transfer the mixture to a strainer set over a large bowl,
and press on it with the back of a spoon, pushing as much
pulp through the strainer as possible. To loosen any pulp
that remains, add the remaining ½ cup water and push again.
When you have pushed as much pulp through the strainer
as possible, scrape whatever is clinging to the bottom of the
strainer into the bowl, wasting nothing. Stir in the lemon
juice and Light Syrup.

7. Preheat the oven to 150 degrees, or to its lowest setting.
Place the cake, still in the pan, on a rimmed baking sheet.
Spoon about ½ cup of the hot syrup over the cake and let it
stand to absorb the syrup. Repeat every 5 to 7 minutes, until
the cake is completely saturated. Pour any syrup that has
spilled onto the baking sheet back into the pan and rewarm
it on top of the stove (or in a bowl in the microwave) as
necessary.

8. Place the cake, still in the pan but removed from the
sticky baking sheet, in the oven and keep it warm until
ready to serve, up to 4 hours.

9. Invert the cake onto a platter; it should fall right out of
the pan. Slice, and serve with the whipped cream.

APPLESAUCE CAKE with POACHED PEARS

Serves 12

FOR THE CRANBERRY SYRUP:

One 12-ounce bag fresh or frozen cranberries

4½ cups water

1½ cups plus 2 tablespoons sugar

6 tablespoons fresh lemon juice

2 cups Light Syrup (page 264)

FOR THE POACHED PEARS:

6 cups robust red wine, such as a Médoc, Cabernet Sauvignon, or Merlot

2 cups water

4½ cups sugar

Six 3-inch cinnamon sticks, crushed

2 tablespoons multicolored whole peppercorns

16 whole cloves

Peeled zest from 2 lemons

Peeled zest from 2 oranges

Placing wine-poached pears on the platter adds more great fall flavor to this dessert, as well as adding beauty to the presentation. The cold vanilla ice cream in the center is a wonderful contrast to the warm cake.

1. Make the cranberry syrup: Combine the cranberries, 4 cups of the water, and the sugar in a medium saucepan and bring to a boil. Turn the heat down to medium-high and cook, stirring occasionally, until the berries stop popping and are very soft and falling apart, about 10 to 15 minutes.

2. Transfer the mixture to a strainer set over a large bowl, and press on it with the back of a spoon, pushing as much pulp through the strainer as possible. To loosen any pulp that remains, add the remaining ½ cup water and push again. When you have pushed as much pulp through the strainer as possible, scrape whatever is clinging to the bottom of the strainer into the bowl, wasting nothing. Stir in the lemon juice and Light Syrup. Set aside. (Cranberry Syrup can be stored in an airtight container in the refrigerator for 2 days.)

3. Poach the pears: Combine the wine, water, sugar, cinnamon sticks, peppercorns, cloves, lemon and orange zest, and raspberries in a medium saucepan and bring to a boil. Strain the liquid into a pot that is just wide enough to hold all of the pears in one layer.

Two 12-ounce bags frozen raspberries

12 small, ripe Bartlett or Anjou pears

----

1 Applesauce Cake (page 54), cooled (still in the pan)

3 tablespoons cornstarch

1 quart Vanilla Ice Cream (page 252) or store-bought vanilla ice cream

4. Cut a round of parchment paper the same size as the poaching pot. Peel and core the pears. Place them in the pot and cover with the parchment, pressing down on the paper to make sure that all the pears are submerged. Bring to a boil and then remove from the heat. Cover the pot and let it stand overnight to cool completely. Remove the parchment after the fruit has cooled. (The pears can be poached several days in advance; cover and refrigerate in the poaching liquid, then bring to room temperature before serving.)

5. Preheat the oven to 150 degrees, or to its lowest setting. Measure out 2 cups of the cranberry syrup and set it aside. Reheat the remaining cranberry syrup. Place the cake, still in the pan, on a rimmed baking sheet. Spoon about ½ cup of the remaining hot syrup over the cake and let it stand to absorb the syrup. Repeat every 5 to 7 minutes, until the cake is completely saturated. Pour any syrup that has spilled onto the baking sheet back into the pan and rewarm it on top of the stove (or in a bowl in the microwave) as necessary.

6. Whisk ½ cup of the reserved cranberry syrup with the cornstarch in a small bowl. Place the remaining 1½ cups reserved cranberry syrup in a small saucepan. Whisk in the cornstarch mixture. Cook over medium heat, whisking constantly, until thickened, 3 to 5 minutes. (The syrup can be prepared up to 2 hours in advance. Keep covered at room temperature.)

(cont. on next page)

7. Place the cake, still in the pan but removed from the sticky baking sheet, in the oven and keep it warm until ready to serve, up to 4 hours.

8. Invert the cake onto a platter; it should fall right out of the pan. Arrange the room-temperature pears around the cake. Spoon the thickened syrup over the cake and pears. Scoop the ice cream into the center of the cake and serve immediately.

APPLESAUCE CAKE with PASTRY LEAVES

Serves 12

FOR THE COOKIES:

4 tablespoons unsalted
butter, softened

$1/2$ cup confectioners' sugar

1 teaspoon pure vanilla
extract

2 teaspoons grated lemon
zest

Pinch salt

2 large egg whites, at room
temperature

$1/3$ cup all-purpose flour

$1/2$ teaspoon unsweetened
cocoa powder

Cranberry syrup (page 56,
Steps 1–2)

1 Applesauce Cake (page 54)

Poached pears (page 56, Steps
3–4), at room temperature

2 pints fresh raspberries,
washed and patted dry

1 cup crème fraîche

To take this cake to the next level, decorate the poached pears by carving their surfaces, blossom end to stem end, with a channel peeler (which can be found in kitchen supply shops and online) before you poach them. This gives the pears a pretty striped design. Then bake some maple leaf–shaped cookies and position them to make it look as if the wind had blown them over the cake. Flutes of cool, crisp Champagne are a must. Happy Holidays!

1. Preheat the oven to 425 degrees. Draw or trace a $2^{1}/_{2}$-inch-long by 2-inch-wide maple leaf onto a thin ($^{1}/_{16}$-inch-thick) piece of clean cardboard. Neatly cut the leaf shape out of the cardboard, forming a stencil.

2. Combine the butter, confectioners' sugar, vanilla, lemon zest, and salt in the bowl of an electric mixer fitted with the paddle attachment. Mix on medium speed until smooth.

3. With the mixer running on medium-high speed, alternately add a tablespoon of egg white and a tablespoon of flour until all of the egg whites and flour have been incorporated and the batter is smooth.

4. Combine $1/2$ cup of the cookie batter and the cocoa powder in a small bowl, and set aside.

(cont. on next page)

5. Line two baking sheets with parchment. Place the stencil in one corner of one of the baking sheets, and drop a tablespoonful of the batter into the leaf cutout. Use a small offset spatula to smooth the batter to the edges of the leaf. Carefully lift the stencil straight up and away from the baking sheet, so that you leave a neat leaf of batter on the parchment. Make 8 batter leaves on the first sheet.

6. Dip the edge of a sharp paring knife into the cocoa batter. Drag the knife edge down the center of a leaf. Drag it from the center to the edges on either side several times, to create veins. Repeat, wiping the knife with a paper towel before redipping it in the cocoa batter, to decorate each leaf. Bake until the edges of the leaves are light brown, 6 to 7 minutes. While the first baking sheet is in the oven, make 8 more batter leaves on the second parchment-lined baking sheet so that they are ready to bake as soon as the first sheet comes out of the oven.

7. When the leaves come out of the oven, immediately pick them up and bend them over the edge of a sheet pan, a rolling pin, and/or a small juice glass to give them a variety of twisted, natural-looking shapes. If they cool too much to be flexible, put them back in the warm oven for 30 seconds to make them pliable, and then continue bending. Let them cool completely. The cooled leaves can be stored in an airtight container at room temperature for up to 2 weeks.

8. Preheat the oven to 150 degrees, or to its lowest setting. Measure out 2 cups of the cranberry syrup and set it aside. Reheat the remaining cranberry syrup. Place the cake, still in the pan, on a rimmed baking sheet. Spoon about ½ cup of the hot syrup over the cake and let it stand to absorb the syrup. Repeat every 5 to 7 minutes, until the cake is completely saturated. Pour any syrup that has spilled onto the baking sheet back into the pan and rewarm it on top of the stove (or in a bowl in the microwave) as necessary.

9. Whisk ½ cup of the reserved cranberry syrup with the cornstarch in a small bowl. Place the remaining 1½ cups reserved cranberry syrup in a small saucepan. Whisk in the cornstarch mixture. Cook over medium heat, whisking constantly, until thickened, 3 to 5 minutes.

10. Place the cake, still in the pan, in the oven and keep it warm until ready to serve, up to 4 hours.

11. Just before serving, invert the cake onto a platter; it should fall right out of the pan. Arrange the pears around the cake. Spoon the thickened syrup over the cake and pears. Fill the center of the cake with the raspberries. Scatter the cookie leaves over the cake and around the platter. Serve immediately, with the crème fraîche on the side.

5. FIRST LADIES' STRAWBERRY CAKE

Although each First Lady I served had her own preferences, every one of them enjoyed this cake and requested it time and again. The classic combination of strawberries and cream is universally appealing, especially when presented in such a pretty package. And I have to admit that it's one of my favorites, too, in part because it lends itself to over-the-top decoration. For the Reverend Billy Graham, I topped the cake with a sugar book opened to the inscription "Happy Birthday." For Laura Bush's birthday, I painted her portrait on a pastillage disk that I then placed on top of the cake. Come to think of it, over the years I painted numerous portraits to top this cake—Mrs. Reagan, James Cagney in the movie *Yankee Doodle Dandy*, Eleanor Roosevelt, and various First Pets including Millie, Barney, Spot, Buddy, and Socks.

SUMMERTIME STRAWBERRY CAKE

Serves 10

6 large eggs

3/4 cup sugar

1 1/4 cups plus 3 tablespoons all-purpose flour

Pinch salt

1/2 tablespoon pure vanilla extract

8 tablespoons (1 stick) unsalted butter, melted

2 pints strawberries, washed, stemmed, and allowed to air-dry

1 cup heavy cream

3/4 cup Grand Marnier or other orange-flavored liqueur

4 cups Pastry Cream (page 249), chilled and strained

1/4 cup cold water

1/2 envelope unflavored gelatin

1/2 cup Light Syrup (page 264)

This was my fallback cake at the White House when I needed something beautiful in a hurry. I could start in the morning and be finished in the early afternoon, knowing I'd have a winner.

1. Preheat the oven to 375 degrees. Grease a 9-inch round cake pan. Line the bottom of the pan with parchment paper, and grease the paper. Dust the pan with flour, and tap out any excess.

2. Pour 2 inches of water into a medium saucepan, and bring to a bare simmer. Combine the eggs and sugar in the bowl of an electric mixer fitted with the whisk attachment. Place the bowl over the simmering water and whisk constantly, by hand or with a handheld mixer, until the egg mixture is just lukewarm to the touch, 86 to 90 degrees on an instant-read thermometer.

3. Return the bowl to the mixer and whisk on high speed for 5 minutes. Then reduce the speed to medium and whisk until the mixture is completely cool, thick, and shiny, another 7 to 8 minutes.

4. Using a rubber spatula, fold in the flour, salt, and vanilla. Spoon about 1 cup of the batter into a small mixing bowl and stir in the butter; then carefully fold the batter-and-butter mixture back into the larger bowl of batter.

5. Pour the batter into the prepared pan and bake until a toothpick inserted into the center comes out clean, 20 to 25 minutes.

6. Remove the pan from the oven and immediately turn the cake out onto a cardboard cake round. Place the round on a wire rack and allow the cake to cool completely.

7. Use a sharp paring knife to stem the strawberries, leaving the stemmed ends flat (don't hull them, in other words).

8. Whip the heavy cream until it just holds stiff peaks.

9. Whisk ½ cup of the Grand Marnier into the strained Pastry Cream.

10. Pour 1 inch of water into a small saucepan and bring to a bare simmer. Place the cold water in a small bowl. Sprinkle the gelatin on top and let stand until dissolved. Then place the bowl over the simmering water and heat, whisking constantly, just until the gelatin melts, 30 seconds to 1 minute.

11. Quickly whisk the gelatin mixture into the Pastry Cream and continue to whisk until smooth. Fold the pastry cream mixture into the whipped cream.

12. Wash and dry the cake pan, and line it with a round of parchment paper. Cut the cake in half horizontally, and place one half in the cake pan. Combine the Light Syrup and the remaining ¼ cup Grand Marnier in a small bowl. Brush the cake layer with half of the Grand Marnier syrup. Spread a ½-inch layer of the cream mixture over the cake. Set aside 2 strawberries for the garnish. Arrange the largest remaining strawberries as close together as possible around the perimeter of the cake so that the flat ends are up against the edge of the cake pan and the pointy ends are

(cont. on next page)

facing the center of the cake. Cut the remaining strawberries in half and arrange them on top of the cream so that they completely cover it. Spread another ¹/₂-inch layer of the cream mixture over the strawberries, making sure to reserve at least ¹/₂ cup of the cream for the top of the cake. Place the second cake layer on top of the cream and brush with the remaining Grand Marnier syrup.

13. Use another cake pan to press down on the cake to compact it. (This will make it easier to slice later on. The large strawberries will be sticking out beyond the cake layers, because the cake will have shrunk during baking and will no longer measure a full 9 inches across.) Cover the cake with plastic wrap and refrigerate it overnight.

14. Unmold the cake by running a sharp paring knife or small offset spatula around the edges and then inverting it onto a cardboard cake round. With a sharp serrated knife, trim all the way around the cake, wiping the knife after every cut, so that the edge is clean and neat. This will give you a very nice strawberry band decoration. Spread the remaining cream mixture over the top of the cake. Slice the reserved berries and garnish with the slices. Serve immediately, or refrigerate for up to 6 hours before serving.

TAILORED STRAWBERRY CAKE

Serves 10

Cornstarch for dusting

1 cup marzipan (see Resources, page 283)

Red food coloring

1 teaspoon corn syrup, if necessary

1 Summertime Strawberry Cake (page 64), without the top layer of cream and the strawberry-slice garnish

12 Tuxedo Strawberries (page 266), leftover dark chocolate reserved for inscribing if desired

This version, decorated with a covering of pleated marzipan, is suitable for a special occasion like an engagement party or a wedding rehearsal dinner. The almond flavor of the marzipan complements the flavors of the cake. It's so much better than the commercial sugar paste that you see on so many bakery cakes these days, recognizable when it gets pushed aside on the plate because it's tasteless. The "tuxedo" strawberries, dipped first in white chocolate and then in dark, add to the cake's formality and its sense of fun. Inscribe a message on the center with leftover dark chocolate if you like. And don't forget the Champagne.

1. Lightly dust the countertop with cornstarch. Place the marzipan on the counter and knead in a drop or two or red food coloring, adding the corn syrup if the marzipan is not soft enough to knead as is. After 30 seconds, your marzipan should be smooth, pliable, and pale pink. Do not overwork the marzipan or it will release its oils and lose its smoothness and pliability.

2. Dust the marzipan and a rolling pin with some more cornstarch, and roll the marzipan out to form a $1/16$-inch-thick round. Trim the round so that it is about $9^1/2$ inches across; you want it to hang over the top of the cake by about an inch.

(cont. on next page)

3. Carefully place the marzipan on top of the cake, letting the extra width hang over the edge by about 1 inch all the way around. (You should be able to see the strawberry layer between the cake layers; if the marzipan covers the strawberries, use sharp scissors to trim it.) Pleat the marzipan edge all the way around so that it looks like a tablecloth hanging off the edge of the table.

4. Place the strawberries around the edge of the cake with the stem ends facing the center. Pipe an inscription with the leftover dark chocolate, if desired (see page 281). Serve immediately, or refrigerate (uncovered) for up to 6 hours before serving.

STRAWBERRY CAKE with A BASKET OF STRAWBERRIES

Serves 10

12 large strawberries with stems, washed and allowed to air-dry

2 cups sugar

1/2 cup water

2 tablespoons light corn syrup

1/4 teaspoon fresh lemon juice

1 Summertime Strawberry Cake (page 64), without the top layer of cream and the strawberry-slice garnish

8 to 10 medium strawberries, washed, stemmed, and allowed to air-dry

Sugar-glazed strawberries and a sugar basket filled with unglazed strawberries make a spectacular presentation for this cake. The basket, although impressive, is actually quite easy to make and can be used on its own, as a container for chocolates or petit fours. Make it up to 2 weeks in advance. To store it, pour about 3 cups of calcium chloride into an airtight container, and cover the calcium chloride with a loose layer of aluminum foil. Set the basket on top of the foil, and seal the container. (Calcium chloride, which you can find at the hardware store, absorbs moisture, allowing the sugar basket to stay shiny and brittle.)

1. Oil two baking sheets, and fill a large bowl with ice water. Set them on the counter.

2. Glaze the large strawberries: Using your hands, stir the sugar and water together in a pot until the mixture is homogeneous. Bring the pot over to the sink. Holding it by the handle with one hand, hold your other hand under the running water from the faucet. With your wet hand, wipe down the sides of the pot until you can't feel any sugar crystals clinging to the sides, rewetting your hand under the running water as necessary.

(cont. on next page)

3. Place the pot on the stove and turn the heat to high. Partially cover the pot so that just some of the steam will be able to escape during cooking. When the mixture comes just to a boil, uncover the pot. Use a long-handled metal spoon to carefully pour the corn syrup into the center of the pot. Do not stir, and do not dribble the syrup onto the sides of the pot. Place the spoon in the center of the pot, resting the handle against the side, and leave it there until all of the corn syrup has dissolved into the sugar mixture, about 1 minute. Then remove the spoon and partially cover the pot again. Allow the mixture to cook, without stirring, until it just begins to take on a little bit of yellow color and registers 308 to 310 degrees on a candy thermometer, 10 to 12 minutes.

4. Remove the pot from the heat. Pour in the lemon juice and shake the pot back and forth until the juice is incorporated. Return the pot to the stove and bring it back to a boil. Continue to cook until the mixture is a very pale yellow and registers 315 degrees on a candy thermometer, about 2 minutes.

5. Remove the pot from the heat and dip the bottom in the ice water to stop the cooking process. Let the sugar mixture stand in the pot for 1 minute to thicken; then remove it from the ice water.

6. Put a folded kitchen towel under one side of the pot so it tilts a bit, letting the sugar pool in the lower portion.

7. Holding a strawberry by its stem, dip it as far as you can into the sugar. Remove any excess by scraping the side of the berry on the edge of the pot. Place the strawberry on one of the prepared baking sheets. Repeat with the remaining strawberries. If the sugar becomes too thick, rewarm it on the stove by moving the pot quickly back and forth across the heat, or put the pot in a 375-degree oven for 5 minutes. (The glazed berries can be kept on the baking sheet for up to 2 hours.)

8. Make the basket: Let the remaining sugar cool slightly in the pot so that it starts to thicken but is still liquid enough to drizzle with a spoon. Oil the inside of a ladle that measures about 3 inches across. Place the ladle in the freezer for 5 minutes. Then remove it from the freezer and drizzle the sugar in a circular motion inside the ladle, covering it entirely. It should almost look like lace. Make sure you drizzle enough sugar so that the resulting bowl will be sturdy. If the sugar in the pot gets too cold or too thick during this process, reheat it over the stove, slowly and continously moving the pan.

9. Wait until the sugar has begun to harden in the ladle but is not completely brittle, just a few seconds. Then slide it out of the ladle, and immediately place it back inside the ladle. This will prevent the sugar basket from sticking to the ladle.

(cont. on next page)

10. Make the foot of the basket by pouring a silver dollar-size round of sugar (it doesn't have to be perfectly round) onto an oiled baking sheet or a Silpat. While the sugar is still warm, push the basket into it, tilting it slightly to one side. Hold it in place while the foot is cooling, about 5 minutes.

11. Make the handle of the basket: Working very quickly so the sugar doesn't have time to harden, drizzle it on the remaining oiled baking sheet, a Silpat, or heavy-duty aluminum foil to form a strip approximately 10 inches long and 1 to 2 inches wide. While the sugar is still soft, cut it into a 10 x 1-inch strip. Bend it into an arc so that the distance between the two ends is the same as the diameter of the basket. You may have to reheat the strip by placing the baking sheet in the oven for a minute to make it pliable enough to bend into shape. Allow the strip to cool completely; then attach the ends to either side of the basket with a dab of leftover sugar.

12. Up to 6 hours before serving, place the basket on the center of the cake and fill with the stemmed unglazed strawberries. (If the weather is very humid, don't fill the basket until right before serving.) Arrange the glazed strawberries around the top perimeter of the cake.

Three Very Different Cheesecakes

The "perfect" cheesecake can mean different things to different people, so over the years I collected the following three recipes to cater to various tastes. The first recipe, for an American-style cheesecake that is baked in a water bath, is more like a custard than an cake, with a rich but not overly heavy consistency that cheesecake-lovers crave. For neat slices, freeze it before cutting and serving it.

The German-style cake is for people who say they don't like cheesecake. It is more cakelike than American-style cheesecake, and is sliced and served at room temperature.

I'm probably most excited about the Coeur à la Crème, a traditional French cheesecake. This is a no-bake cake that is molded in a heart-shaped pan and refrigerated until firm. Served with fresh fruit, it is fresh and light, more like a cheese course than a cake. I think it's the ultimate summer dessert—easy to make, refreshing on the palate, and transportable in its mold to a picnic or an outdoor party.

6. AMERICAN-STYLE CHEESECAKE

I like a very creamy, delicately textured cheesecake that's neither too heavy nor insubstantially fluffy. After years of tinkering, I came up with a formula that's just right for me. Cream cheese gives the cake its characteristic tangy flavor, and heavy cream makes it tender like a custard. For the neatest slices, cut it while it is still frozen and let the individual slices defrost on the plates before serving.

AMERICAN-STYLE CHEESECAKE with FRUIT SAUCE

Serves 12

FOR THE CAKE:

Four 8-ounce packages Philadelphia brand cream cheese, softened

1¼ cups sugar

1 teaspoon grated lemon zest

½ teaspoon grated orange zest

5 large eggs, at room temperature

2 large egg yolks, at room temperature

½ tablespoon pure vanilla extract

1 cup heavy cream

TO FINISH:

1 recipe Chunky Strawberry Sauce (page 263), Raspberry Sauce (page 261), or Mango Sauce (page 264)

This cheesecake has no crust, which cuts down on the work and also makes the cake extra-creamy. I like to cut the richness of the cake by serving it with a fruit sauce. Strawberry, Raspberry, and Mango Sauces all work well; the choice depends on the availability of the fruit and your personal taste. This cheesecake was a standby at large White House receptions, presliced and placed next to bowls containing different fruit sauces. That way, people moving down the buffet line could serve themselves a slice and then choose their own garnish.

1. Position a rack in the middle of the oven, and preheat the oven to 350 degrees. Place a 10-inch round of parchment in the bottom of a 10-inch round cake pan.

2. Combine the cream cheese, sugar, lemon zest, and orange zest in the bowl of an electric mixer fitted with the paddle attachment. Mix on low speed until smooth. Add the eggs, and then the yolks, one at a time, scraping down the sides of the bowl after each addition. Mix in the vanilla. Mix in the heavy cream, ½ cup at a time, scraping down the sides of the bowl after each addition. The mixture should be very smooth.

3. Place the cake pan on a rimmed baking sheet or shallow baking pan. Pour the filling into the cake pan. Carefully pour ½ inch of very hot tap water into the baking sheet. Bake until the cheesecake is still jiggly in the center but set around the edges, about 1 hour. Remove it from the oven, discard the water bath, and allow the cheesecake to cool completely in the pan on a wire rack.

4. When the cake has cooled completely, wrap it in plastic and place it in the freezer overnight. (Cheesecake, still in the pan, can be wrapped in plastic and then foil and frozen for up to 2 months.)

5. Remove the cake from the freezer. Run the bottom of the pan over a gas burner for several seconds to loosen the cake from the pan. (Alternatively, dip the pan in a bowl of hot water for 1 minute.) Run a sharp paring knife around the edges of the pan. Cover the top of the pan with plastic wrap and invert a plate over the plastic. Invert, and shake gently to release the cake. Invert a serving platter on top of the released cake and invert it again so that the cake is right side up.

6. Slice the cake, and let the slices stand for 30 minutes. Garnish the individual slices with your choice of fruit sauce, and serve.

CREAM CHEESE FLOATING ISLAND

Serves 12

Red food coloring

1 recipe Vanilla Sauce (page 251), chilled

¼ cup Grand Marnier or other orange-flavored liqueur

1 American-Style Cheesecake (page 76), frozen and still in the pan

2 cups fresh blueberries, washed and patted dry

2 cups fresh raspberries

Fresh mint leaves for garnish

When the Reagans arrived at the White House, one of the first edicts I received from Mrs. Reagan was "absolutely no cheesecake." I kept a few in the freezer to serve when I knew the First Lady wouldn't be around for dessert, but I was careful never to break one out when she was in the vicinity. One day I got an order at the very last minute for a ladies' luncheon dessert and all I had on hand was cheesecake! Thinking quickly, I grabbed an ice cream scoop and shaped the cheesecake into ovals and set the pretty shapes on top of a platter of orange-flavored vanilla sauce. A sprinkling of berries for flavor and color finished the dessert beautifully. Holding my breath, I listened at the dining room door for the response. I heard plenty of oohs and aahs from Mrs. Reagan and her friends, and received many compliments later. After that lunch, cheesecake was still banned from Mrs. Reagan's table, but Cream Cheese Floating Island was requested often. It just goes to show how a creative presentation can persuade even the pickiest eaters to try something they think they won't like!

1. Whisk a drop or two of red food coloring into the Vanilla Sauce to turn it a pale orange color. Whisk in the Grand Marnier.

2. Pour the sauce onto a large rimmed serving platter so that it covers the entire platter.

3. Use an oval ice cream scoop to scoop 12 ovals from the frozen cheesecake. Arrange the ovals on the platter.

4. Scatter the berries around the floating islands. Garnish the platter with fresh mint leaves, and serve immediately.

CHEESECAKE with GANACHE

Serves 12

1 American-Style Cheesecake (page 76), frozen and still in the pan

1 recipe Ganache (page 258), lukewarm

Tuxedo Strawberries (page 266, optional)

Lukewarm ganache spreads beautifully and firms up quickly on a still-frozen cheesecake. The "tuxedo" strawberries are optional, but they do turn the cake into a black tie–worthy dessert.

1. Remove the cake from the freezer. Run the bottom of the pan over a gas burner for several seconds to loosen the cake from the pan, or dip it in a bowl of hot water for 1 minute. Run a sharp paring knife around the edges of the pan. Cover the top of the pan with plastic wrap and invert a plate over the plastic. Invert, and shake gently to release the cake. Invert a large serving platter on top of the released cake and invert it again so that the cake is right side up.

2. Using a small offset spatula, spread the ganache over the top of the cake. Let it stand until the ganache is set, about 15 minutes.

3. While the cake is still semifrozen, use a sharp chef's knife to cut it into slices, dipping the knife into hot water and wiping it dry before making each slice. Let the slices stand for at least 30 minutes and up to 1 hour before serving.

4. Serve with Tuxedo Strawberries on the side, if desired.

7. AN UNUSUAL CHEESECAKE

This is a German recipe that I learned as a young pastry assistant in Hamburg. I took it everywhere with me—Paris, London, Bermuda, and finally the U.S. Unlike creamy New York– or Italian-style cheesecakes, where the emphasis is on the cheese, this German-style version is a true cake. The half cup of flour that is added to the batter gives it a cakelike crumb when baked. It doesn't freeze as well or keep as long as traditional cheesecake (this just means it will stay fresh for 2 to 3 days instead of 10). But it travels better, since it can stay out of the refrigerator for 2 days.

GERMAN CHEESE PIE

Serves 8

1½ cups graham cracker crumbs (from about 13 whole graham crackers)

3 tablespoons plus ¼ cup sugar

12 tablespoons (1½ sticks) unsalted butter, melted and slightly cooled

One 8-ounce package Philadelphia brand cream cheese, at room temperature

6 tablespoons sour cream

½ teaspoon finely grated lemon zest

1 teaspoon pure vanilla extract

¼ cup all-purpose flour

3 large eggs, separated

6 tablespoons milk

Pinch salt

1 cup strained apricot jam

Three 15-ounce cans apricot halves in syrup, drained and patted dry; or four 11-ounce cans mandarin oranges in syrup, drained and patted dry

¼ cup coarsely chopped unsalted pistachio nuts

The pie is the most casual shape for this dessert. It's great for backyard barbecues and other informal summer entertaining. Graham cracker crusts are typically American, so I always use them, even in my German cheesecakes. Canned apricot halves are deliciously sweet and tart on top of the pie. Mandarin oranges are also very pretty and tasty.

1. Preheat the oven to 375 degrees. Combine the graham cracker crumbs, the 3 tablespoons sugar, and the butter in a medium mixing bowl and stir until the crumbs are moistened.

2. Press the mixture evenly over the bottom and all the way up the sides of a 9-inch pie plate, packing it tightly with your fingertips so it is even and compacted.

3. Combine the cream cheese, sour cream, and remaining ¼ cup sugar in the bowl of an electric mixer fitted with the paddle attachment, and mix on medium-low speed until very smooth and creamy. Add the lemon zest and vanilla, and mix to incorporate. Beat in the flour until the mixture is smooth. Add the egg yolks, one at a time, and beat until smooth. Stir in the milk.

4. In a clean bowl, whip the egg whites and salt on high speed with the whisk attachment until they are shiny and just hold stiff peaks. Gently but thoroughly fold the cream cheese mixture into the egg whites.

5. Scrape the batter into the prepared crust and bake until a toothpick inserted into the center comes out clean, 20 minutes. Let the pie cool completely on a wire rack.

6. Spread ¼ cup of the jam over the top of the pie. Arrange the apricot halves, rounded side up, on top of the jam. Place the remaining ¾ cup jam in a small saucepan and heat it just to a boil. Brush the hot jam liberally over the apricots. Sprinkle the nuts over the apricots.

7. Serve immediately, store in a cake dome at room temperature for up to 2 days, or store, covered with plastic wrap, in the refrigerator for up to 1 week.

LACY GERMAN CHEESECAKE with FRUIT SAUCE

Serves 10 to 12

FOR THE CHEESECAKE:

2 cups graham cracker crumbs

5 tablespoons plus ½ cup granulated sugar

1 cup (2 sticks) unsalted butter, melted and slightly cooled

Two 8-ounce packages Philadelphia brand cream cheese, at room temperature

¾ cup sour cream

2 teaspoons pure vanilla extract

1 teaspoon grated lemon zest

½ cup plus 1 tablespoon all-purpose flour

6 large egg yolks

½ cup plus 2 tablespoons milk

5 egg whites

Pinch salt

TO FINISH:

2 tablespoons confectioners' sugar

1 recipe Raspberry Sauce (page 261), Orange Sauce (page 263), or Chunky Strawberry Sauce (page 263)

This recipe contains some unusual directions but they make perfect baking sense. If you simply bake the cake straight through, it will rise too high, and then the top will crack and the cake will fall. Removing it from the oven midway slows down its rise (it continues to bake on the counter, but much less slowly), so this won't happen.

1. Preheat the oven to 425 degrees. Combine the graham cracker crumbs, the 5 tablespoons sugar, and the butter in a medium mixing bowl and stir until the crumbs are moistened. Press the mixture evenly across the bottom and up the sides of a 9-inch springform pan, packing it tightly with your fingertips so it is evenly compacted.

2. Combine the cream cheese, sour cream, and remaining ½ cup sugar in the bowl of an electric mixer fitted with the paddle attachment, and mix on medium-low speed until very smooth and creamy. Stir in the vanilla and lemon zest. Beat in the flour until the mixture is smooth. Add the egg yolks, one at a time, and beat until smooth. Stir in the milk.

3. In a clean bowl, whip the egg whites and salt on high speed with the whisk attachment until they are shiny and just hold stiff peaks. Gently but thoroughly fold the cream cheese mixture into the egg whites.

4. Pour the batter into the pan and bake until the cake starts to rise and the top just begins to brown, about 30 minutes. Remove it from the oven. Insert a paring knife, at a 45 degree angle, between the edge of the cake and the pan.

Run the knife around the edge of the pan to release the cake from the sides and prevent the top from cracking as the cake cools and shrinks. Let it stand on a wire rack for 30 minutes.

5. Lower the oven temperature to 350 degrees. Put the cake back in the oven and continue to bake until it has risen about 1 inch in the pan, 20 minutes. Let it cool completely on a wire rack.

6. Release the sides of the springform pan, and store the cake under a cake dome at room temperature for up to 2 days, or refrigerate it for up to 1 week.

7. Just before serving, place an 8-inch round paper doily on top of the cake and dust it heavily with the confectioners' sugar. Remove the doily carefully, so as not to disturb the design. Slice, and serve with your choice of fruit sauce on the side.

EMBELLISHED CHEESECAKE

Serves 8 to 10

FOR THE LANGUE DE CHAT PETALS:

4 tablespoons unsalted butter, softened

1/2 cup confectioners' sugar

1 teaspoon pure vanilla extract

2 teaspoons grated lemon zest

Pinch salt

2 large egg whites, at room temperature

1/3 cup all-purpose flour

TO ASSEMBLE THE CAKE:

1 cup red currant jelly

German Cheesecake (page 84), cooled and unmolded (refrigerated for up to 3 days)

2 cups fresh blueberries, washed and patted dry

1/2 small cantaloupe, scooped into pearl-size balls with the smallest size melon baller

12 large strawberries, washed, stemmed, allowed to air-dry, and scooped into pearl-size balls just like the cantaloupe

The cake is transformed into a beautiful edible flower in this version. "Petals" made of langue de chat cookies ring the edge, and blueberries, along with tiny balls of cantaloupe and strawberries, form the center. Use the tiniest melon baller you can find to cut the melon and the strawberries—you want balls about the same size as the blueberries. As they say in Germany, *"Sehr gemutlich!"* (Have fun!)

1. Make the langue de chat petals: Preheat the oven to 425 degrees. On a thin (1/16-inch-thick) piece of clean cardboard, draw a triangle with one side measuring 1 1/2 inches and the other two sides measuring 2 1/2 inches. Neatly cut out the triangle to form a stencil.

2. Combine the butter, confectioners' sugar, vanilla, lemon zest, and salt in the bowl of an electric mixer fitted with the paddle attachment. Mix on medium speed until smooth.

3. With the mixer running on medium-high speed, alternately add a tablespoon of egg white and a tablespoon of the flour until all of the egg whites and flour are incorporated and the batter is smooth.

4. Line a baking sheet with parchment. Place the stencil in one corner of the baking sheet and drop about 1 1/2 teaspoons of the batter into the cutout triangle. Use a small offset spatula to smooth the batter to the edges of the cutout. Carefully lift the stencil straight up and away from the baking sheet so that you leave a neat triangle of batter on

the parchment. Make 19 more batter triangles on the same sheet. Bake until the edges of the triangles are light brown, 6 to 7 minutes.

5. When the triangles come out of the oven, immediately lift them from the baking sheet, and using an offset spatula and your finger, drape them over the side of a juice glass or rolling pin to form curved petal shapes. Let them cool completely before transferring them to an airtight container. (They can be stored in the container at room temperature for 3 to 4 days.)

6. Assemble the cake: Place the jelly in a bowl and stir to loosen it. Release the sides of the springform pan and place the cake on a serving platter. Use an offset spatula to spread a thin layer of the jelly over the top of the cake.

7. Arrange the langue de chat cookies around the edge of the cake so they look like flower petals.

8. In a medium bowl, combine the blueberries, cantaloupe, and strawberries with the remaining jelly and toss gently to coat. Mound the fruit in the center of the cake so it looks like the center of the flower. Serve immediately, or store under a cake dome at room temperature for up to 2 hours before serving.

8. COEUR À LA CRÈME

This is a traditional French dessert, a simple cheesecake made by draining a mixture of sweetened cream cheese and crème fraîche of excess moisture in a special heart-shaped ceramic mold with holes in the bottom. These molds can be found in cookware shops and online (see Resources, page 283). As with baked cheesecakes, the best way to ensure that you have a smooth dessert is to bring the cream cheese to room temperature and beat it well before mixing it with the other ingredients. When finished, the coeur is a pure white heart, ready to decorate in a variety of ways. At the White House, I changed its presentation for Valentine's Day, Mother's Day, and many other occasions, using a variety of fresh fruits in season to brighten and enhance it, and even decorating it with finely piped chocolate when I was feeling artistic.

COEUR à la CRÈME with BLUEBERRY SAUCE

Serves 6 to 8

FOR THE COEUR À LA CRÈME:

14 ounces Philadelphia brand cream cheese, at room temperature

6 tablespoons granulated sugar

Pinch salt

1¹/₃ cups crème fraîche

TO FINISH:

1 recipe Blueberry Sauce (page 262)

¹/₂ cup fresh blueberries for garnish

Blueberry sauce and some fresh blueberries garnish this simple cake. If you are serving this for Valentine's Day and would like to add a touch of red, scatter some raspberries around the cake along with the blueberries.

1. Wet a 15 x 15-inch piece of cheesecloth with cold water and wring out so it is damp but not dripping. Place the cheesecloth inside a 9-inch coeur à la crème mold, with the edges overhanging the rim of the mold. Place the mold on a rimmed baking sheet.

2. Place the cream cheese, sugar, and salt in the bowl of an electric mixer fitted with the paddle attachment, and beat until fluffy. In another bowl, whip the crème fraîche with the whisk attachment until it just holds stiff peaks. Gently fold the crème fraîche into the cream cheese mixture.

3. Scrape the mixture into the cheesecloth-lined mold and smooth it with a spatula. Fold the overhanging cheesecloth on top of the mixture, smoothing out the wrinkles where possible, so that its surface is completely covered. Gently pat it down. Refrigerate the mold, still on the baking sheet, overnight to allow the excess moisture to drain.

4. Peel away the cheesecloth that covers the top, and invert the mold onto a serving platter. Lift off the mold and carefully peel away and discard the cheesecloth. Spoon the sauce around the cake, and let it stand for 30 minutes. Garnish with the fresh blueberries, and serve.

COEUR à la CRÈME with HONEY VANILLA SAUCE and FRESH FRUIT

Serves 6 to 8

FOR THE HONEY VANILLA SAUCE:

1/2 cup honey

5 large egg yolks

2 cups half-and-half

1 vanilla bean, split lengthwise

---

1 Coeur à la Crème (page 90), drained and chilled, still in the mold

1 ripe mango, peeled, pitted, and cut into thin slices

1/2 pint fresh raspberries

1 recipe Raspberry Sauce (page 261)

2 ripe kiwis, peeled and thinly sliced

Honey Vanilla Sauce adds a delicate flavor and aroma, as well as sweetness, to this dessert. For the most aromatic sauce, seek out beautifully scented honey from an artisan producer (I use lavender honey from a local apiary).

1. Make the Honey Vanilla Sauce: Whisk the honey and egg yolks together in a medium bowl. Combine the half-and-half and the vanilla bean in a heavy saucepan, and bring to a boil.

2. Slowly dribble 1/4 cup of the hot half-and-half into the egg yolk mixture, whisking constantly. Dribble another 1/4 cup of the half-and-half into the egg yolk mixture, again whisking constantly. Then whisk the egg yolk mixture back into the remaining half-and-half and return the pan to the heat. Cook over low heat, stirring constantly with a wooden spoon or a rubber spatula, until the mixture shows the first sign of coming to a boil. Quickly strain the sauce into a bowl, and refrigerate until cold.

3. Peel away the cheesecloth that covers the top of the Coeur à la Crème and invert the mold onto a large serving platter. Lift off the mold and carefully peel away and discard the cheesecloth.

4. Arrange the mango slices and raspberries around the cake. Drizzle the Honey Vanilla Sauce, and then the Raspberry Sauce, around the fruit so that strands of the drizzled sauces artfully intertwine. Arrange the kiwi slices around the perimeter of the platter. Let stand 30 minutes before serving.

CHOCOLATE ARTIST'S COEUR à la CRÈME

Serves 6 to 8

1 Coeur à la Crème (page 90), drained and chilled, still in the mold

¹/₂ cup semisweet chocolate chips

A few drops of warm water

¹/₂ cup apricot jam, strained

Green food coloring

1 ripe mango, peeled, pitted, and cut into thin slices

¹/₂ pint fresh raspberries

1 recipe Honey Vanilla Sauce (page 91)

1 recipe Raspberry Sauce (page 261)

2 ripe kiwis, peeled and thinly sliced

Here is a challenge for people who love to decorate: Use a cornet, a small cone made of parchment paper, to pipe a fine chocolate design of leaves and flowers over your Coeur à la Crème. Let your decorations harden in the refrigerator; then garnish the cake with the fruit and sauces just before serving. The cornet technique can be used on many cakes. If you've never done it, melt extra chocolate and practice on a sheet of parchment paper before you begin to decorate your cake. I use jam to fill in the petals and leaves with some color. It works just as well as commercial piping jelly but tastes much better.

1. Peel away the cheesecloth that covers the top of the Coeur à la Crème, and invert the mold onto a large serving platter. Lift off the mold and carefully peel away and discard the cheesecloth.

2. Place the chocolate chips in a heatproof bowl and melt in a microwave or over simmering water. Stir in a couple of drops of warm water, until the mixture has the consistency of a smooth paste. Make a cornet (see page 281) and scrape the melted chocolate mixture into it. Cut a pinhole-size opening in the tip with sharp scissors. Test by writing on a piece of parchment. Then, holding the cone at a 90-degree angle about 1 inch above the cake, pipe a design of vines. Outline some flowers and leaves along the vines. The chocolate will set immediately.

3. Make two more cornets. Divide the jam between two bowls, and color one bowl of jam with a few drops of green food coloring. Scrape the jams into the cornets. Cut openings in the cornets and fill in the petals with the orange jam and the leaves with the green jam.

4. Arrange the mango slices and raspberries around the cake. Drizzle the Honey Vanilla Sauce, and then the Raspberry Sauce, around the fruit so that strands of the drizzled sauces artfully intertwine. Arrange the kiwi slices around the perimeter of the platter. Let stand 30 minutes before serving.

Delicious Dairy- and Wheat-Free Cakes

I t was always an interesting challenge when a new family moved into the White House and I had to adjust my baking style to fit a new set of likes and dislikes. When the Carters left and the Reagans moved in, I started to make many more sorbet and fresh fruit desserts, because that is what Mrs. Reagan liked. Every day I baked a selection of light, delicate cookies for the family to snack on. The Bush family had a different set of preferences. Mrs. Bush didn't want the grandkids snacking on cookies all day, so I didn't bake them as often, and if there were any leftovers from an event, I locked them up. Unlike Mrs. Reagan, Mrs. Bush was partial to crème brûlée and other custard desserts, so I had to dust off those recipes at the start of the new administration.

Even more challenging were the dietary restrictions of family members and guests. If an incoming President had food allergies or other dietary requirements, his personal physician would meet with me on Inauguration Day to go over the details. And of course the rules of diplomacy, not to mention hospitality, required that I honor any religious dietary restrictions of foreign visitors: Desserts for Muslim guests never contained alcohol. Israeli State Dinners were strictly kosher.

I always did my best to make desserts that could be served to everybody at the table, so the person who couldn't eat wheat (President Clinton among them) or dairy would not feel isolated. At the same time, I was determined that no matter what the constraints, the desserts I served wouldn't be compromised in flavor. In fact, many times I designed wonderful new desserts that I might not have tried had I not been faced with restrictions, and went on to serve these same desserts to audiences who had no special dietary needs at all. I created each one of the following cakes to satisfy a special dietary requirement. The Orange Sherbet Cake was designed for the State Dinner in honor of the prime minister of Israel. The Carrot Cake and the Pineapple Cake, both wheat-free, were made for President Clinton. The Apricot Soufflé Cake dates back to the first Bush administration, when some of the President's grandchildren couldn't eat wheat. I continued to make each one because it was a hit with guests who were not on restricted diets.

9. ORANGE SHERBET CAKE

I came up with this cake early in my White House years,
when President and Mrs. Carter hosted Israeli Prime Minister
Menachem Begin. Dessert had to be kosher, meaning it couldn't
contain any dairy since it would be served after a meal that
included meat. I settled on a genoise filled with orange sorbet.
Oranges are a major crop in Israel, and that way the cake
would honor the guest's home country. Making dessert for
the Israeli prime minister involved a lot more than choosing
the right ingredients, however. For the first and only time, a
team of rabbis visited the White House kitchens. They covered
the wooden tables with aluminum foil so the food on top of
the table would not be contaminated with non-kosher food
prepared earlier. Then workers came in and used a propane
torch to cleanse the oven, cooktop, counters, pots, pans,
and every other piece of equipment that would touch the
food. China and silverware were boiled in stockpots. Under
the watchful eye of Rabbi Caviar, I got to work early in the
morning a few days before the dinner. As I cracked eggs into
a bowl, he checked every one of them for a spot of blood. At
around 10 a.m. he casually asked me where I kept the Grand
Marnier. I told him that all the liqueurs were in a distant
storeroom but that I wouldn't need it until later, for the sauce.
He asked again an hour later, so I brought him the bottle and

continued working on the cakes. The rabbi poured himself a glass to enjoy as he trailed me around the kitchen, and we proceeded very pleasantly. By the afternoon, I was back in the storeroom again for another bottle, this time for the sauce!

As I pulled together the ingredients for the sorbet, there was one glitch. In those days I didn't have my own ice cream freezer at the White House and the rabbi insisted that I make the sorbet in a machine that had never been used before. I called a prominent Washington restaurant because I knew the chef had just gotten a new machine, and he agreed to let me churn my sorbet over there. I arrived at the restaurant early the next morning in the White House car, and Jean-Louis himself showed me the brand-new ice cream maker. As soon as I was done I returned to the White House to fill the cakes with the freshly churned sorbet. Even though *The Washington Post* reported that the sorbet for the State Dinner came from the big restaurant, I knew that the dessert was all mine. And I had the sweet satisfaction of hearing from the butler that Prime Minister Begin had said the Orange Sherbet Cake was the best kosher dessert he had ever had. It was quite a compliment so early in my tenure at the White House.

I garnished the State Dinner version with spectacular glazed orange segments and an orange and apricot sauce. But simpler versions are refreshing and fun for less formal occasions. Eating a slice of Simplest Orange Sherbet Cake is almost like eating an ice cream sandwich.

SIMPLEST ORANGE SHERBET CAKE

Serves 12

FOR THE CAKE:

4 large eggs

½ cup sugar

¾ cup plus 1½ tablespoons all-purpose flour

Pinch salt

1 teaspoon pure vanilla extract

FOR THE SORBET:

3½ cups strained fresh orange juice

½ cup strained fresh lemon juice

1 cup sugar

The cake can be made in advance and frozen for up to 1 month, but the sorbet must be soft and freshly churned when you put the dessert together.

1. Make the cake: Preheat the oven to 375 degrees. Grease a 9 x 2-inch-deep round cake pan. Dust the pan with flour, and tap out any excess.

2. Pour 2 inches of water into a medium saucepan and bring to a bare simmer. Combine the eggs and sugar in the bowl of an electric mixer fitted with the whisk attachment. Place the bowl over the simmering water and whisk constantly, by hand or with a handheld mixer, until the egg mixture is just lukewarm to the touch, 86 to 90 degrees on an instant-read thermometer.

3. Return the bowl to the mixer and whisk on high speed for 5 minutes. Then reduce the speed to medium and whisk until the mixture is completely cool, thick, and shiny, another 12 minutes.

4. Using a rubber spatula, fold in the flour, salt, and vanilla.

5. Pour the batter into the prepared pan and bake until a toothpick inserted into the center comes out clean, 20 to 25 minutes.

(cont. on next page)

6. Remove the pan from the oven and immediately turn the cake out onto a cardboard cake round. Place the round on a wire rack and allow the cake to cool completely. (The cake can be wrapped in plastic wrap and then in aluminum foil and frozen for up to 1 month; defrost it overnight in the refrigerator before using it.)

7. Make the sorbet: Combine the orange juice, lemon juice, and sugar in a bowl and stir to dissolve the sugar. Let stand for 15 minutes and then stir again, making sure that all of the sugar has dissolved. Freeze in an ice cream maker according to the manufacturer's instructions.

8. While the sorbet is churning, wash and dry the cake pan and line it with parchment paper. Using a sharp serrated knife, slice the genoise in half horizontally. Place the bottom half in the pan, and spread the sorbet evenly over it. Place the top half of the cake on top of the sorbet, and press on it lightly. Wrap the cake in plastic wrap and freeze until it is very firm, at least 2 hours and up to 1 day.

9. To unmold, run a sharp paring knife around the edges of the cake. Invert a serving platter over the pan and turn them over, shaking gently to release the cake. Peel away the parchment paper. Slice and serve.

Genoise

The Orange Sherbet Cake, First Ladies' Strawberry Cake, Upside-Down Cake, and several others in this book all use genoise, or sponge cake, as a base. Genoise is an important cake layer in the baker's canon because it provides structure and at the same time melds well with other cake components. Butter cakes can't absorb as much syrup as genoise; filled, frosted, and refrigerated, even very moist butter cakes will taste dry when sliced and served. Buttercream frosting, hardened in the refrigerator, will fall off butter cakes in large chunks instead of adhering to the surface, as it does with genoise. Genoise layers, on the other hand, soak up syrup and stay moist in the refrigerator for days (but don't freeze soaked genoise, or the cake will become icy). Feather-light, they support any filling—whipped cream, mousse or Bavarian cream, buttercream, ganache, ice cream, sorbet, you name it—without making the cake heavy. For flavor, pastry chefs often choose genoise. Unlike butter cake, which has a distinctly buttery flavor, genoise is a chameleon, able to take on the flavors of the soaking syrup, filling, and frosting instead of competing with them. Genoise itself can also be flavored with cocoa powder or espresso powder to complement chocolate- or coffee-flavored fillings and frostings.

ORANGE SHERBET CAKE with WHIPPED TOPPING

Serves 12

2 cups heavy cream, chilled, or one 16-ounce container nondairy whipped topping

3 tablespoons confectioners' sugar (if using cream)

1 teaspoon pure vanilla extract (if using cream)

1 Simplest Orange Sherbet Cake (page 99), frozen for at least 2 hours or up to 24 hours, still in the pan

12 orange segments, white pith removed (from about 2 navel oranges)

This cake is easy to dress up with piped whipped cream. (To keep it kosher, use nondairy whipped topping.) Orange segments surrounding the decorated cake finish the presentation. To pipe whipped cream, use a very big star tip, which makes the job quicker. Squeezing it through a smaller tip will deflate the cream.

1. Place the cream in the bowl of an electric mixer fitted with the whisk attachment, and whip on high speed until soft peaks appear. Add the confectioners' sugar and vanilla, and continue to whip until the cream just holds stiff peaks. Do not overwhip. (If using nondairy whipped topping, there's no need to whip it or to add the sugar and vanilla.) Use immediately, or cover with plastic wrap and refrigerate for up to 2 hours.

2. Unmold the cake by running a sharp paring knife around the edges of the pan. Invert a serving platter over the pan and turn them over, shaking the pan gently to release the cake. Peel away the parchment paper.

3. Spread a ¼-inch-thick layer of the whipped cream topping over the top of the cake, using a small offset spatula. Fit a pastry bag with a #6 or #8 star tip, fill it with the remaining whipped cream topping, and pipe rows of stars on the sides of the cake, working from the bottom to the top. Pipe large rosettes all around the top edge of the cake. (The decorated cake can be frozen for up to 1 week: First freeze it, uncovered, for several hours until firm. Then wrap it in plastic wrap and store it in the freezer.)

4. When you are ready to serve it, place the orange segments, one end resting on a rosette, all around the cake. Slice the cake so that each slice contains an orange section, and serve immediately.

ORANGE SHERBET CAKE with GLAZED ORANGES

Serves 12

FOR THE GLAZED
ORANGES:

3 navel oranges

2 cups sugar

½ cup water

2 tablespoons light corn
syrup

¼ teaspoon fresh lemon juice

Red food coloring

FOR THE SAUCE:

2 large navel oranges

1 cup apricot jam

½ cup Grand Marnier or other
orange-flavored liqueur

2 cups heavy cream, chilled,
or one 16-ounce container
nondairy whipped topping

3 tablespoons confectioners'
sugar

1 teaspoon pure vanilla
extract

1 Orange Sherbet Cake (page
99), frozen for at least 2
hours or up to 24 hours, still
in the pan

Here is the State Dinner version of this dessert, complete with sugar-glazed orange segments and the Grand Marnier sauce for a spectacular finish. Boiling the oranges briefly makes it easy to peel them; the skins and pith will come away cleanly. If you find that some segments are too small to use, just discard them. Make sure to leave the segments to dry overnight, as described, so that the sugar will dry and set properly. Again, if you want to keep it kosher, substitute the nondairy whipped topping for the whipped cream.

1. Make the glazed orange segments: One day before you plan to serve the cake, bring a large pot of water to a boil. Drop the (unpeeled) oranges into the water and boil for 3 to 4 minutes. Remove them from the water and let them stand until they are cool enough to handle. Then peel the oranges and divide them into segments, pulling them apart without breaking the membranes. Line a baking sheet with a clean kitchen towel. Place the segments on the towel, narrow sides up, and let them stand overnight. The next day they should have a hard, dry skin.

2. On serving day, oil a baking sheet, and fill a large bowl with ice water. Set them on the counter.

3. Using your hands, stir the sugar and water together in a saucepan until the mixture is homogeneous. Bring the pan over to the sink. Holding it by the handle with one hand, hold your other hand under the running water from the faucet. With your wet hand, wipe down the sides of the pan until you can't feel any sugar crystals clinging to the sides, rewetting your hand under the running water as necessary.

4. Place the pan on the stove and turn the heat to high. Partially cover the pan so that some of the steam will be able to escape during cooking. When the mixture comes just to a boil, uncover the pot. Use a long-handled metal spoon to carefully pour the corn syrup into the center of the pan. Do not stir, and do not dribble the syrup onto the sides of the pan. Place the spoon in the center of the pan, resting the handle against the side, and leave it there until all of the corn syrup has dissolved into the sugar mixture, about 1 minute. Then remove the spoon and partially cover the pan again. Allow the mixture to cook, without stirring, until it just begins to take on a little bit of yellow color and registers 308 to 310 degrees on a candy thermometer, 10 to 12 minutes.

5. Remove the pan from the heat. Pour in the lemon juice and shake the pan back and forth until the juice is incorporated. Return the pan to the stove and bring it back to a boil. Continue to cook until the mixture is a very pale yellow and registers 315 degrees on a candy thermometer, about 2 minutes.

(cont. on next page)

6. Remove the pan from the heat and dip the bottom in the ice water to stop the cooking process, about 1 minute. Then put a folded kitchen towel under one side of the pot so it tilts a bit, letting the thickened sugar pool in the lower portion.

7. Dip an orange segment halfway into the sugar. Scrape the bottom of the segment on the edge of the pan to remove any excess, and place the dipped segment on the prepared baking sheet. Repeat with the remaining segments. If the sugar becomes too thick, rewarm it on the stove by moving the pan quickly back and forth across the heat, or put the pan in a 375-degree oven for 5 minutes.

8. When all the segments have been dipped halfway, stir a few drops of red food coloring into the remaining sugar mixture. Dip the uncoated half of each segment in the red sugar, scraping them on the edge of the pan as before. Let the orange segments cool on the baking sheet. Use immediately, or let stand (uncovered) for up to 8 hours on a dry day. (On a humid day, the sugar will begin to dissolve more quickly.)

9. Make the sauce: Peel and segment the oranges, removing as much of the white pith as you can. Cut the segments into 1/4-inch cubes. Place the fruit and any juice in a small bowl, and stir in the jam and Grand Marnier. If the sauce tastes too sweet, add water, 1 tablespoon at a time, to correct it. Let stand at room temperature until ready to use.

10. Put the cake together: Place the cream in the bowl of an electric mixer fitted with the whisk attachment, and whip on high speed until soft peaks appear. Add the confectioners' sugar and vanilla, and continue to whip until the cream just holds stiff peaks. Do not overwhip. Use immediately, or cover with plastic wrap and refrigerate for up to 2 hours.

11. Unmold the cake by running a sharp paring knife around the edges of the pan. Invert a serving platter over the pan and turn them over, shaking the pan gently to release the cake. Peel away the parchment paper.

12. Spread a ¼-inch-thick layer of whipped cream over the top of the cake, using a small offset spatula. Fit a pastry bag with a #6 or #8 star tip, fill it with the remaining whipped cream, and pipe rows of stars on the sides of the cake, working from the bottom to the top. Pipe large rosettes all around the top edge of the cake.

13. Just before serving, arrange the glazed orange segments on top of the cake. Slice, and serve with the sauce on the side.

10. CARROT CAKE MADE WITH SPELT

One of President Clinton's favorite cakes was carrot cake, so I made this wheat-free version often for him. Made with vegetable oil instead of butter and served with sorbet instead of ice cream, it is also relatively low in cholesterol—ideal for people concerned about cardiac health.

CARROT CUPCAKES

Makes 24 cupcakes

FOR THE CUPCAKES:

1½ cups spelt flour

½ cup cornstarch

2 teaspoons baking soda

1 teaspoon salt

1 teaspoon ground cinnamon

4 large eggs, at room temperature

1½ cups canola or sunflower oil

1½ teaspoons pure vanilla extract

2 cups sugar

3 cups shredded carrots

1 cup coarsely chopped pecans

FOR THE TOPPING:

One 12-ounce jar apricot jam, strained

1½ cups cubed canned pineapple, drained and patted dry

1 carrot, peeled and finely shredded with a lemon zester or a Microplane grater

2 tablespoons finely chopped crystallized ginger

Serve these for brunch or lunch. For a casual dessert, add whipped cream or vanilla ice cream.

1. Preheat the oven to 350 degrees. Line two 12-cup muffin tins with paper liners.

2. Combine the spelt flour, cornstarch, baking soda, salt, and cinnamon in a medium bowl.

3. Place the eggs, oil, vanilla, and sugar in the bowl of an electric mixer fitted with the whisk attachment, and whisk on high speed until the mixture resembles a runny mayonnaise, about 5 minutes. Stir in the flour mixture until just combined. Stir in the carrots and pecans.

4. Divide the batter among the muffin cups, and bake until a toothpick inserted into the center of a muffin comes out clean, 18 to 20 minutes. Cool the muffins in the pan for about 5 minutes. Then invert the muffins onto a rack, re-invert them onto another rack so they are right side up, and allow to cool completely.

5. Combine the jam and the pineapple in a medium bowl, and toss until the pineapple is completely coated. Spoon some pineapple mixture on top of each cupcake.

6. Combine the shredded carrot and crystallized ginger in a small bowl. Place a pinch of the mixture on top of each cupcake. Serve immediately.

Cake into Cupcakes

A couple of cake batters in this book, in addition to the Carrot Cake, make especially fine cupcakes:

To make Banana Cupcakes, spoon Banana Cake batter into two 12-cup muffin tins lined with paper liners. Bake at 375 degrees until a cake tester or toothpick comes out clean, 18 to 20 minutes. Once the cupcakes are cool, whip together 8 tablespoons (1 stick) softened unsalted butter, 6 ounces (¾ bar) of softened cream cheese, and 2 tablespoons strawberry preserves until smooth; spread this frosting over the cupcakes. Press about 1 tablespoon of corn, bran, or wheat flake cereal into the frosting on each muffin just before serving.

To make Chocolate-Frosted Yellow Cupcakes, spoon Yellow Cake batter into two 12-cup muffin tins lined with paper liners. Bake at 375 degrees until a cake tester or toothpick comes out clean, 18 to 20 minutes. Once the cupcakes are cool, spread some Ganache (see page 258) over the tops and sprinkle with chopped unsalted peanuts.

WARM CARROT CAKE with PINEAPPLE-CARROT SORBET

Serves 12

FOR THE SORBET:

1/2 large pineapple, peeled, cored, and cut into chunks

2 cups fresh carrot juice

1 to 1 1/4 cups sugar, to taste

1/4 cup fresh lemon juice

Red food coloring

FOR THE CAKE:

3/4 cup spelt flour

1/4 cup cornstarch

1 teaspoon baking soda

1/2 teaspoon salt

1/2 teaspoon ground cinnamon

2 large eggs, at room temperature

3/4 cup canola or sunflower oil

1 teaspoon pure vanilla extract

1 cup sugar

1 1/2 cups shredded carrots

1/2 cup coarsely chopped pecans

The combination of warm cake with icy-cold sorbet is wonderful. I challenge anyone to come up with a more refreshing and unusual wheat- and dairy-free dessert.

1. Make the sorbet: Puree the pineapple, in batches, in a blender, and then push the puree through a strainer into a bowl. Measure out 2 cups of puree; reserve any extra for another use.

2. Combine the pineapple puree, carrot juice, sugar, lemon juice, and a drop or two of food coloring in a bowl and stir to dissolve the sugar. Let stand for 15 minutes. Then stir the mixture and freeze it in an ice cream maker according to the manufacturer's instructions. Scrape the sorbet into an airtight container and freeze it until ready to serve, up to 1 week.

3. Make the cake: Preheat the oven to 350 degrees. Grease and flour a 9-inch round cake pan.

4. Combine the spelt flour, cornstarch, baking soda, salt, and cinnamon in a medium bowl.

5. Place the eggs, oil, vanilla, and sugar in the bowl of an electric mixer fitted with the whisk attachment, and whisk on high speed until the mixture resembles a runny mayonnaise, about 5 minutes. Stir in the flour mixture until just combined. Stir in the carrots and pecans.

TO FINISH:

Confectioners' sugar for
dusting

6. Scrape the batter into the prepared pan and bake until
a toothpick inserted into the center of the cake comes
out clean, about 30 minutes. Cool in the pan for about 10
minutes. Then invert the cake onto a wire rack, and invert it
again onto a platter so it is right side up. Dust the cake with
confectioners' sugar, slice, and serve warm, with the sorbet
on the side.

FROZEN CARROT and PINEAPPLE CAKE

Serves 12

FOR THE SORBET:

½ large pineapple, peeled, cored, and cut into chunks

2 cups fresh carrot juice

1 to 1¼ cups sugar, to taste

¼ cup fresh lemon juice

Red food coloring

FOR THE CAKE:

1 Carrot Cake (page 112), baked, turned out onto a cardboard cake round, and cooled completely (the cooled cake can be wrapped in plastic wrap and held at room temperature for 1 day, or in the freezer for up to 2 weeks)

TO FINISH:

½ cup strained apricot jam

1½ recipes Sweetened Whipped Cream (page 248)

Carrot Cake won't get rock-hard in the freezer, so it makes a beautiful frozen dessert, especially when covered with whipped cream. Bake the cake and let it cool completely. Don't make the sorbet until you are ready to put the cake together; it should be fresh and soft, so it will spread easily over the layers.

1. Make the sorbet: Puree the pineapple, in batches, in a blender, and then push the puree through a strainer into a bowl. Measure out 2 cups of puree; reserve any extra for another use.

2. Combine the pineapple puree, carrot juice, sugar, lemon juice, and a drop or two of food coloring in a bowl and stir to dissolve the sugar. Let stand for 15 minutes. Then stir the mixture and freeze it in an ice cream maker according to the manufacturer's instructions.

3. While the sorbet is churning, use a sharp serrated knife to cut the cake in half horizontally. Wash and dry the cake pan, and line it with a round of parchment paper. Place one cake layer in the pan and spread a 1½-inch layer of sorbet on top of the layer (reserve any leftover sorbet for another use). Place the second cake layer on top of the sorbet. Place the pan in the freezer for 30 minutes to firm up.

4. Place the apricot jam in a pastry bag fitted with a small plain tip.

5. Run a sharp paring knife around the edges of the cake and invert it onto a serving platter. Peel away the parchment.

6. Smooth about two thirds of the whipped cream over the top and sides of the cake. Quickly, before the cream has hardened, pipe horizontal lines of the apricot jam, ¼ inch apart, over the top of the cake. Run a knife through the whipped cream, making vertical lines ¾ inch apart, to make a pattern in the jam.

7. Scrape the remaining whipped cream into a pastry bag fitted with a large star tip, and pipe rosettes around the top edge of the cake. Pipe scallops along the bottom edge. Let the cake stand at room temperature for 15 minutes to allow the sorbet to soften. Then slice and serve. (Or freeze the cake until the whipped cream is firm, about 30 minutes; then wrap the cake in plastic and put it back in the freezer for up to 3 weeks.)

Lance Armstrong's Paris Brest

Tailored Strawberry Cake

Cherry Almond Trifle Cake

Hazelnut Ring Tea Cake with
Caramelized Phyllo Dough

Rubies and Gold Dome Cake

Pineapple-Meringue Cake
with Mango Sauce

Bûche de Noël with Marzipan Squirrels,
Meringue Mushrooms and Chocolate Bark

11. WHEAT-FREE PINEAPPLE CAKE

During the Clinton administration I developed many special desserts for the President, who is allergic to wheat. The genoise that forms the base of this cake can be made with spelt flour and a little bit of cornstarch instead of all-purpose flour. Even if you don't have food allergies, this cake is well worth trying for its powerful pineapple flavor, which is concentrated when the fruit is caramelized. If possible, buy a golden pineapple from Costa Rica. It is reliably flavorful and sweet, while other pineapples are hit or miss.

CARAMELIZED PINEAPPLE CAKE

Serves 12

FOR THE CAKE:

4 large eggs

1/2 cup granulated sugar

3/4 cup plus 1 1/2 tablespoons all-purpose flour; or 3/4 cup spelt flour plus 3 tablespoons cornstarch, sifted together

Pinch salt

1 teaspoon pure vanilla extract

1 large fresh pineapple, preferably a golden Costa Rica pineapple

1 3/4 cups water

2 cups granulated sugar

4 tablespoons unsalted margarine

1/2 cup (packed) light brown sugar

1/2 cup honey

1/2 cup cream of coconut, such as Coco Lopez

1 teaspoon pure vanilla extract

President Clinton especially liked boldly flavored cakes, and I designed this one, with pineapple, rum, and passion fruit juice, with his tastes in mind. It also has no pastry cream, buttercream, or other creamy filling, which I avoided when making cakes for him. Most pineapple cakes are made with canned pineapple, but I use fresh here because it won't fall apart while it is cooked (cooking pineapple brings out its flavor and sweetness).

1. Preheat the oven to 375 degrees. Grease a 9 x 2-inch-deep round cake pan. Line the bottom of the pan with parchment paper, dust it with flour, and tap out any excess.

2. Pour 2 inches of water into the bottom of a double boiler or into a medium saucepan, and bring to a bare simmer. Combine the eggs and sugar in the bowl of an electric mixer fitted with the whisk attachment. Place the bowl over the pan of simmering water and whisk constantly, by hand or with a handheld mixer, until the egg mixture is just lukewarm to the touch, about 86 to 90 degrees on an instant-read thermometer.

3. Transfer the bowl to the mixer and whisk on high speed for 5 minutes. Then reduce the speed to medium and whisk until the mixture is completely cool, thick, and shiny, another 12 minutes.

3 tablespoons dark rum

1 cup passion fruit juice

One 12-ounce jar apricot jam, strained

2 cups sliced almonds, toasted until golden and then lightly crushed

4. Using a rubber spatula, fold in the flour (or spelt and cornstarch), salt, and vanilla. Pour the batter into the prepared pan and bake until a toothpick inserted into the center comes out clean, 20 to 25 minutes. Remove the pan from the oven and immediately turn the cake out onto a cardboard cake round. Place the round on a wire rack and let the cake cool completely. (The cake can be wrapped in plastic wrap and then foil and frozen for up to 1 month. Defrost it overnight in the refrigerator before using.)

5. Cut a slice on the top of the pineapple, removing the leaves and rind. Stick a fork in the core so you have something to hold on to, and pare the rind away in thin vertical strips, taking care not to lose too much flesh. Slice off the end. Cut three ½-inch-thick rounds from the top of the pineapple, and remove the core from each slice with a small biscuit cutter (about the same diameter as a wine bottle cork). Cut the remaining pineapple in half and then remove the woody core by making a V-shaped cut around the center of each half. Cut the cored pineapple into 1-inch pieces.

6. Combine 1½ cups of the water and the granulated sugar in a medium saucepan and bring to a boil. Place the 3 pineapple rings in the pan, cover, lower the heat, and cook at a bare simmer until tender, about 45 minutes. Remove the pan from the heat and let the pineapple cool in the syrup; then refrigerate, still in the syrup.

(cont. on next page)

7. Measure out 4 cups of the cut-up pineapple pieces (reserve any remaining pineapple for another use). Combine the butter, light brown sugar, honey, cream, vanilla, and rum in a large, heavy frying pan. Turn the heat to high and bring to a boil. Add the pineapple pieces and cook over high heat, shaking the pan frequently, until the pineapple is just beginning to soften, no more than 3 to 4 minutes. Use a slotted spoon to transfer the caramelized pineapple pieces to a rimmed baking sheet or large plate.

8. Continue to cook the caramel in the pan until it reaches the soft ball stage, about 238 degrees on a candy thermometer. (To test without a thermometer, spoon a tiny bit of the caramel into a glass of ice water. You should be able to form a very soft ball from the caramel at this stage.) Remove the pan from the heat and let the caramel stand in the pan for 5 minutes to thicken slightly.

9. Using a sharp serrated knife, cut the cake into two horizontal layers. Leave one layer on the cardboard round and brush half of the passion fruit juice over it.

10. Stir the caramelized pineapple pieces back into the caramel. If the caramel is too thick to mix, stir in some of the syrup from the chilled pineapple rings until it is loose enough to coat the pineapple. Carefully arrange the caramelized pineapple pieces over the cake layer, scraping all the caramel out of the pan and drizzling it evenly over the pineapple. Place the second cake layer over the pineapple and press it down lightly. Brush the top cake layer with the remaining passion fruit juice.

11. Heat the jam and the remaining ¼ cup water in a small saucepan. Brush the hot jam over the top and sides of the cake, and then press the almonds into the sides. Pat the pineapple slices dry, and place one in the center of the cake. Cut the 2 remaining slices into 12 pieces each, and arrange the pieces all around the top edge of the cake. Serve immediately, or drape with plastic wrap and refrigerate for up to 1 day before serving.

PINEAPPLE-MERINGUE CAKE

Serves 12

6 large egg whites

1½ cups granulated sugar

1 Caramelized Pineapple Cake (page 118), assembled but without the apricot jam glaze and toasted almond coating

2 slices store-bought green candied pineapple, cut into 1-inch pieces

2 slices store-bought yellow candied pineapple, cut into 1-inch pieces

2 tablespoons confectioners' sugar

Meringue frosting is a dairy-free alternative to whipped cream. I use Swiss Meringue, for which you warm the egg whites and sugar over a bowl of simmering water as you whip them. Heating the mixture like this makes it more stable, so it stays beautiful, and also gives it a beautiful shine. For the finishing touch, confectioners' sugar is sifted over the top and then caramelized in the oven.

1. Preheat the oven to 425 degrees. Combine the egg whites and the granulated sugar in the bowl of an electric mixer fitted with the whisk attachment. Pour 2 inches of water into a saucepan, and bring to a full boil. Place the mixing bowl over the pan of boiling water and whisk constantly, by hand or with a handheld mixer, until the egg whites feel like warm soup to the touch, about 125 degrees on an instant-read thermometer.

2. Transfer the bowl to the mixer and whisk on high speed until the meringue is cool and stiff.

3. Place the cake on a baking sheet. Use an offset spatula to cover the cake with some of the meringue, forming a smooth layer. Scrape the remaining meringue into a pastry bag fitted with a #6 or #8 star tip, and pipe rosettes around the top edge of the cake. Place alternating green and yellow pieces of candied pineapple in front of each rosette.

4. Dust the top of the cake with the confectioners' sugar, put it in the oven, and bake until the meringue is browned, 1 to 2 minutes. Stay right by the oven and keep a close eye on it, to make sure you pull it out before the meringue begins to burn. Let the cake cool on the counter briefly, then serve immediately. (Or drape the cake with plastic wrap and refrigerate for up to 6 hours; let it come to room temperature before serving.)

PINEAPPLE-MERINGUE CAKE FANTASY

Serves 12

6 large egg whites

1½ cups granulated sugar

1 Caramelized Pineapple Cake (page 118), assembled but without the apricot jam glaze and toasted almond coating

2 tablespoons confectioners' sugar

¾ cup strained apricot jam

2 tablespoons water

Reserved leaves from the pineapple

Give this cake a spectacular garnish by piping some meringue on top of it in the shape of a pineapple, using the reserved pineapple leaves to decorate it. It is a tropical delight, welcome in the middle of winter as well as in the summer.

1. Preheat the oven to 425 degrees. Combine the egg whites and the granulated sugar in the bowl of an electric mixer fitted with the whisk attachment. Pour 2 inches of water into a saucepan and bring to a full boil. Place the mixing bowl over the pan of boiling water and whisk constantly, by hand or with a handheld mixer, until the egg whites feel like warm soup to the touch, about 125 degrees on an instant-read thermometer.

2. Transfer the bowl to the mixer and whisk on high speed until the meringue is cool and stiff.

3. Place the cake on a baking sheet. Use an offset spatula to cover the cake with some of the meringue, forming a smooth layer. Spoon some more meringue onto the center of the cake in a mounded oval shape, resembling a pineapple half. Scrape the remaining meringue into a pastry bag fitted with a #7 or #8 star tip, and pipe stars all over the mound to resemble the skin of the pineapple.

4. Dust the top of the cake with the confectioners' sugar, put it in the oven, and bake until the meringue is browned, 1 to 2 minutes. Stay right by the oven and keep a close eye on it, to make sure you pull it out before the meringue begins to burn. Transfer the cake to a serving platter.

5. Heat the jam and water in a small saucepan until the mixture is warm and pourable. Brush the jam mixture over the meringue pineapple. Arrange the leaves so that they look as if they are growing from the pineapple top.

6. Serve immediately, or refrigerate (uncovered) for up to 6 hours before serving.

12. APRICOT SOUFFLÉ CAKE

Soufflés were always popular at the White House, and I was always experimenting with techniques for making fruit soufflés with a rich flavor. Pureeing some rehydrated dried apricots one day, I noticed how intense their flavor was and how little liquid they released, compared to fresh fruit. So I added them to a soufflé and was amazed at the powerful fruit flavor of the dessert. That might have been the end of the story, but one morning I came in to work and saw some leftover soufflés, still in their dishes, from the night before. I turned them over, planning to clean up, and was surprised at how the deflated soufflés held their shape—just like cake layers. Taking a taste, I realized that a new cake had just been born! Not only that, but it was a wheat-free cake, something I was always looking for to serve to the many people on restricted diets who passed through the White House dining rooms.

APRICOT SOUFFLÉ CAKE with APRICOT GRAND MARNIER SAUCE

Serves 10

FOR THE CAKE:

1/2 cup granulated sugar, plus more for sprinkling

1 pound dried apricots

2 teaspoons fresh lemon juice

1 teaspoon grated lemon zest

5 large egg whites, at room temperature

2 tablespoons confectioners' sugar

FOR THE SAUCE:

2 cups apricot preserves, strained

1/3 cup Grand Marnier or other orange-flavored liqueur

2/3 cup water

TO FINISH:

Mint sprigs

Crème fraîche (optional)

A heavy ceramic soufflé dish is the key piece of equipment for this cake. It retains heat and conducts it slowly through the cake batter, so that the inside and outside of the cake are done at the same time. If this cake is baked in a metal pan, it will burn on the outside before the batter at the center can cook through.

1. Preheat the oven to 375 degrees. Butter a heavy ceramic 4- to 5-cup soufflé dish, 9 or 10 inches in diameter and 3 inches deep, and sprinkle with granulated sugar.

2. Place the apricots in a medium saucepan, cover with cold water, and bring just to a boil. Lower the heat and cook, covered, at a bare simmer until tender, 30 to 40 minutes.

3. Drain the apricots and puree them in a food processor. Measure out 1 1/2 cups of the puree, reserving any extra for another use. Combine the pureed apricots, 1/4 cup of the granulated sugar, the lemon juice, and the lemon zest in a large bowl.

4. Place the egg whites in the bowl of an electric mixer fitted with the whisk attachment, and beat on high speed until they form soft peaks, adding the remaining 1/4 cup sugar in a slow stream. Continue to beat until the egg whites hold very stiff peaks. Stir half of the egg whites into the apricot mixture to lighten it. Then fold the remaining egg whites into the apricot mixture, being careful not to deflate the whites.

5. Pour the mixture into the soufflé dish, smooth the top with a spatula, and sift the confectioners' sugar over the top. Run the tip of your thumb around the inside edge of the soufflé dish to wipe it clean, ensuring the highest rise. Bake until firm and well risen, 30 to 35 minutes. Remove the soufflé from the oven and let it stand on a wire rack until cool and deflated, 20 to 30 minutes.

6. Make the sauce: Combine the apricot preserves, Grand Marnier, and water and mix until smooth.

7. Invert a serving dish on top of the soufflé dish, turn them over, and shake gently to release the cake. Pour the Grand Marnier Sauce over the cake. Slice and serve, with a sprig of mint and a spoonful of crème fraîche if desired.

APRICOT SOUFFLÉ CAKE with HONEY MERINGUE

Serves 10

FOR THE CAKE:

1/2 cup granulated sugar, plus more for sprinkling

1 pound dried apricots

2 teaspoons fresh lemon juice

1 teaspoon grated lemon zest

5 large egg whites, at room temperature

1 tablespoon dry unseasoned bread crumbs or cake crumbs

FOR THE SAUCE:

2 cups apricot preserves, strained

1/3 cup Grand Marnier or other orange-flavored liqueur

1/2 cup water

FOR THE MERINGUE:

5 large egg whites, at room temperature

1 cup clover honey

1 cup sweetened flaked coconut

TO FINISH:

2 tablespoons confectioners' sugar

When frosting the Apricot Soufflé Cake, I choose honey meringue instead of whipped cream, to keep the cake dairy-free as well as wheat-free. The meringue topping gives you that lush, creamy effect without using cream. The flavor of honey is particularly good with the acidic apricots. A little coconut stirred into some of the meringue creates a nicely textured filling for this two-layered version.

1. Preheat the oven to 375 degrees. Butter two 9-inch round soufflé dishes with 3-inch sides, and sprinkle with granulated sugar.

2. Place the apricots in a medium saucepan, cover with cold water, and bring just to a boil. Lower the heat and cook, covered, at a bare simmer until tender, 30 to 40 minutes.

3. Drain the apricots and puree them in a food processor. You should have about 1 cup. Combine the pureed apricots, 1/4 cup of the granulated sugar, the lemon juice, and the lemon zest in a large bowl.

4. Place the egg whites in the bowl of an electric mixer fitted with the whisk attachment, and beat on high speed until they form soft peaks, adding the remaining 1/4 cup sugar in a slow stream. Continue to beat until the egg whites hold very stiff peaks. Stir half of the egg whites into the apricot mixture to lighten it. Then fold the remaining egg whites into the apricot mixture, being careful not to deflate the whites.

5. Divide the mixture between the two soufflé dishes, and smooth the tops with a spatula. Run the tip of your thumb around the inside edge of each soufflé dish to ensure the highest rise. Bake until firm and well risen, about 20 minutes.

6. Remove the dishes from the oven and let stand on a wire rack until cool and deflated. When the layers are completely cool, invert a heatproof serving platter over one of the dishes and invert the soufflé onto it. Sprinkle the bread crumbs over the other layer, place a cardboard cake round on top, and invert.

7. Make the sauce: Combine the apricot preserves, Grand Marnier, and water in a bowl, and stir until smooth.

8. Make the meringue: Place the egg whites in the bowl of an electric mixer fitted with the whisk attachment.

9. Place the honey in a small, deep saucepan and cook over medium-high heat, watching carefully so that it doesn't boil over, until it reaches the soft ball stage, 240 degrees on a candy thermometer.

10. Turn the mixer on high and pour the honey into the egg whites in a slow, steady stream, making sure that none of it falls on the whisk. Continue to whip on high speed until the meringue holds stiff peaks and is almost cool.

11. Preheat the oven to 450 degrees.

(cont. on next page)

12. Scrape one third of the meringue into a medium bowl, and stir in the coconut. Smooth the coconut meringue over the top of the layer on the serving platter.

13. Carefully slide the remaining layer on top of the meringue. Reserve 2 cups of the meringue. Smooth the remaining meringue over the top and sides of the cake. Scrape the reserved meringue into a pastry bag fitted with a large star tip, and pipe stars all over the top of the cake.

14. Dust the top of the cake with confectioners' sugar, put it in the oven, and bake until browned, about 1 minute. Watch the cake carefully and turn it if necessary for even coloring. Let the cake cool, and serve with the Apricot Grand Marnier Sauce on the side.

APRICOT SOUFFLÉ CAKE with STRAWBERRY COMPOTE

Serves 10

FOR THE STRAWBERRY COMPOTE:

1/2 cup cold water

2 cups granulated sugar

2 1/2 cups fresh strawberries, washed and stemmed (about 2 pounds, 6 ounces without the stems)

Red food coloring

3 tablespoons fresh lemon juice

1 tablespoon Sure-Gel

One 2-layer Apricot Soufflé Cake (page 128), prepared through Step 6

FOR THE MERINGUE:

4 large egg whites, at room temperature

3/4 cup plus 2 tablespoons (10 ounces) clover honey

1 cup sweetened flaked coconut

TO FINISH:

2 tablespoons confectioners' sugar

This version, topped with a fruity strawberry compote, is fantastic and the colors are beautiful. Sure-Gel, a brand of fruit pectin used to make jams and jellies, is available at the supermarket; you'll find it next to the gelatin. It thickens up the berries without making them gelatinous.

1. Make the strawberry compote: Combine the cold water and 1 1/2 cups of the sugar in a large saucepan and bring to a boil, stirring occasionally to dissolve the sugar. Lower the heat, add the strawberries and a few drops of red food coloring, and cook at a bare simmer until the berries are just beginning to soften, 8 to 10 minutes. Pour about one third of the cooking liquid into a bowl, and stir in the Sure-Gel and the remaining 1/2 cup sugar. Stir the mixture back into the pan, bring to a simmer, and cook for 1 minute. Scrape the compote into a bowl, cover with plastic wrap, and refrigerate overnight.

2. Make the cake.

3. Make the meringue: Place the egg whites in the bowl of an electric mixer fitted with the whisk attachment.

4. Place the honey in a small, deep saucepan and cook over medium-high heat, watching carefully so that it doesn't boil over, until it reaches the soft ball stage, 240 degrees on a candy thermometer.

(cont. on next page)

5. Turn the mixer on high and pour the honey into the egg whites in a slow, steady stream, making sure that none of it falls on the whisk. Continue to whip on high speed until the meringue holds stiff peaks and is almost cool.

6. Preheat the oven to 450 degrees. Scrape one third of the meringue into a medium bowl, and stir in the coconut. Smooth the coconut meringue over the top of the cake layer on the serving platter.

7. Carefully slide the remaining layer on top of the meringue. Reserve about 1 cup of the meringue. Smooth the remaining meringue over the top and sides of the cake. Scrape the reserved meringue into a pastry bag fitted with a large star tip, and pipe stars around the top edge of the cake.

8. Dust the top of the cake with confectioners' sugar, put it in the oven, and bake until browned, about 1 minute. Watch the cake carefully and turn it if necessary for even coloring. Let cool.

9. Add the lemon juice to the compote. Spoon the compote over the top of the cake. Serve immediately, or let stand (uncovered) at room temperature for up to 2 hours before serving.

Nuts, Chocolate, and Coffee

I 've had the opportunity to observe thousands of people as they eat dessert, and I would say that the ones who prefer nuts, chocolate, and coffee to fresh fruit are a breed of their own. This group doesn't just enjoy these ingredients—they crave them.

The following cakes will satisfy the cravings of all types of eaters. The Mousse-Filled Chocolate Soufflé Cake is the lightest of chocolate cakes, but with enough intense chocolate flavor to please the chocoholic. The Classic Hazelnut Dacquoise employs the incomparable duo of chocolate and hazelnuts. The Rubies and Gold Dome Cake is filled with white chocolate mousse and covered with chocolate's favorite fruit, the raspberry. And the Hazelnut Ring Cake with Caramelized Phyllo combines nuts, chocolate, and coffee for people who like their dessert pleasures in threes.

13. HAZELNUT RING CAKE

I often made this buttery, delicious cake for White House teas and receptions. The rich flavor of the hazelnut buttercream and the delightful crunch of the praline topping make it a satisfying afternoon treat. President Reagan especially liked "the crunchy cake," as he called it. He requested it for his birthday several times, so I developed a dressed-up version in his honor, which you'll find on page 142.

HAZELNUT RING TEA CAKE

Serves 12

FOR THE CAKE:

1 cup plus 2 tablespoons all-purpose flour

1 teaspoon baking powder

Pinch salt

2 large eggs, at room temperature

3/4 cup sugar

1 tablespoon pure vanilla extract

4 tablespoons unsalted butter, melted and cooled

1/2 cup crème fraîche or sour cream, at room temperature

1/2 cup hazelnut praline paste (see Resources, page 283)

3 1/2 cups French Buttercream (page 254)

1 recipe Nougat (page 265), crushed

Crème fraîche gives this cake a welcome acidity, balancing the sweetness of the sugar and the praline paste. Substitute sour cream if you prefer. Use a light touch when putting this cake together; overmixing will make it greasy and heavy. You may have some leftover buttercream, but it's always better to have too much than too little. It can be difficult to spread frosting smoothly over the rounded top of a bundt cake with an offset spatula, so I use this trick: After spreading the frosting all over the cake with the spatula, I cut a strip of parchment paper about 8 inches long and 1 inch wide. Holding an end in each hand, I form the strip into a horseshoe shape, the same shape as the top of the cake. Then I pull the edge of the paper horseshoe along the top of the cake, all around, to smooth out the frosting.

1. Make the cake: Preheat the oven to 400 degrees. Heavily grease and flour an 8-inch tube pan.

2. Stir the flour, baking powder, and salt together in a small bowl.

3. In a large bowl, combine the eggs, sugar, and vanilla. Stir until well combined, but do not overmix. Stir the flour mixture into the egg mixture. Then stir in the butter and crème fraîche.

4. Pour the batter into the prepared pan, and bake until the cake begins to form a crust, about 15 minutes. Without opening the oven door, turn the heat down to 350 degrees and continue baking until a toothpick inserted into the

center comes out clean, 20 to 30 minutes longer. Let the cake rest in the pan on a wire rack for 5 minutes. Then invert the cake onto a wire rack and unmold it. Re-invert it onto another wire rack so it is right side up, and allow it to cool completely.

5. Whisk the praline paste into the buttercream until smooth.

6. Using a sharp serrated knife, slice the cake horizontally into three equal layers. Wash and dry the tube pan, and place the top cake layer back in the pan. Fit a pastry bag with a plain #6 tip, fill it with some of the buttercream, and pipe a ½-inch-thick layer of buttercream over the cake layer in the pan. Place the middle cake layer on top of the buttercream, and press on it lightly with your fingers so the cake comes in full contact with the buttercream. Pipe another ½-inch layer of buttercream over the second cake layer. Place the bottom cake layer on top of this layer of buttercream, pressing down again. Cover the pan with plastic wrap and freeze it for 1 hour. (The cake can be frozen for up to 3 months. Defrost it in the refrigerator overnight before proceeding with the recipe.)

7. To unmold the cake, dip the pan in a bowl of hot water for 30 seconds; then invert it onto a cardboard cake round, shaking it once or twice to release it.

8. Use a small offset spatula to spread the remaining buttercream all over the cake. Pull the edge of a strip of parchment paper along the top of the cake to smooth the frosting (see the headnote). Press the nougat all over the cake just before serving.

CHOCOLATE-GLAZED HAZELNUT RING CAKE

Serves 12

1 Hazelnut Ring Tea Cake (page 138), without buttercream frosting and nougat garnish

1 recipe Semisweet Chocolate Glaze (page 260), at room temperature

Italians have two separate names for hazelnut and chocolate-hazelnut gelato—*nocciola* and *gianduia*—to distinguish the two, because adding chocolate to hazelnut utterly transforms its flavor. The difference is comparable to the difference between this hazelnut ring cake, simply glazed with chocolate, and the previous version; they're related but have distinct personalities.

1. Place a wire rack in a rimmed baking sheet. Place the cake on the rack.

2. Pour the glaze into a large measuring cup and drizzle it over the entire cake, coating it completely. Let the cake stand until the glaze is set, about 20 minutes. Scrape the glaze that has drizzled onto the baking sheet back into the measuring cup.

3. Just before serving, heat the reserved glaze in the microwave so that it is warm, and serve it on the side with slices of the cake.

Phyllo

Phyllo, the tissue-thin Greek pastry, has many uses beyond the traditional baklava. By itself it doesn't have much flavor, but when brushed with butter and sprinkled with sugar, it caramelizes and becomes deliciously buttery and crunchy. I make small cups with it, molded in muffin tins, to hold fruit and ice cream; I make larger cups to hold baked apples; and I use it to make pastry domes that cover ice cream bombes.

Phyllo is not difficult to work with, as long as you don't let it dry out. Unroll the dough on the countertop and cover it with a damp (but not wet) kitchen towel. Remove the sheets one at a time as you work, always replacing the towel. Whatever shape I'm making, I never use more than 3 or 4 sheets of the dough, so that my containers and covers are delicate and easy to eat.

Try to buy your phyllo dough at a Greek market, where it is sold fresh from the refrigerator case. It will keep in your refrigerator unopened for up to a month, but once you open it, use it within a day or two, before it starts to dry out. I prefer fresh dough to frozen dough (which is sold in most supermarkets) because I've found that the frozen leaves of phyllo dough often stick to each other, crumbling to pieces instead of separating neatly. If this happens, don't throw the dough out. Brush it with melted butter, sprinkle it with sugar, and bake it until it is golden; then break up the pieces once they have cooled, and store them in an airtight container at room temperature. Use these phyllo pieces as you would use toasted chopped nuts to garnish cakes.

HAZELNUT RING CAKE with CARAMELIZED PHYLLO

Serves 12

4 sheets phyllo dough
(thawed if frozen)

6 tablespoons unsalted
butter, melted and slightly
cooled

9 tablespoons sugar

1 tablespoon instant espresso
powder

1 tablespoon hot water

2 recipes Sweetened Whipped
Cream (page 248)

1 Chocolate-Glazed Hazelnut
Ring Cake (page 140)

1 tablespoon unsweetened
cocoa powder

To transform the ring cake into a birthday dessert for President Reagan, I filled the center with espresso-flavored whipped cream and shards of caramelized phyllo. The phyllo is also used to create a fan decoration for the top of the cake. A dusting of cocoa powder completes the spectacular presentation. Phyllo dough is available in the refrigerator or freezer section of the supermarket. Make the cake in advance, bake the phyllo in advance, but assemble the cake at the last minute, or the phyllo will get soggy.

1. Preheat the oven to 375 degrees. Lay 1 sheet of phyllo dough on a baking sheet, and brush about 2 tablespoons of the butter over it. Sprinkle with 3 tablespoons of the sugar. Repeat with 2 more sheets of phyllo, stacking them on top of one another. Place the fourth sheet on top, but do not brush it with butter or sprinkle it with sugar.

2. Bake the phyllo until it is dark golden, 6 to 8 minutes. Don't underbake, or it will get soggy later on, but watch carefully, because soon after the phyllo caramelizes, it will start to burn. Remove it from the oven and let the phyllo cool completely on the baking sheet.

3. Combine the espresso powder and hot water in a small bowl, and stir to dissolve. Fold the mixture into the whipped cream.

4. Break up the cooled phyllo into uneven pieces, reserving 7 or 8 of the most attractive pieces for decoration.

5. Spoon about ½ cup of the whipped cream into the center of the ring cake. Top with some phyllo shards. Continue to layer this way until you have no whipped cream and phyllo left and have reached the top of the ring.

6. Arrange the reserved pieces of phyllo in a fan shape on top of the whipped cream (see photo insert). Dust the cake with the cocoa powder, and serve.

14. VERY VERSATILE HAZELNUT DACQUOISE

This dacquoise (a cake consisting of meringue layers made with hazelnut flour and hazelnuts) offers the baker a lot of flexibility. It can be baked briefly so it is soft and yielding, or kept in the oven longer so it comes out crisp and crunchy. Because hazelnuts pair well with a variety of flavors, it can be filled with almost anything: ganache, pastry cream, buttercream, fruit filling. To bring out the hazelnut flavor, toast the flour as well as the hazelnuts before mixing the cake batter (see page 149).

CLASSIC HAZELNUT DACQUOISE

Serves 12

1 cup hazelnut flour, toasted (see page 149)

1½ cups granulated sugar

2 tablespoons all-purpose flour

5 tablespoons whole milk

8 large egg whites, at room temperature

2 cups hazelnuts, skinned (see page 151) and coarsely chopped

2 tablespoons confectioners' sugar

1 recipe Vanilla Sauce (page 251), freshly made and still hot

4 ounces bittersweet chocolate, finely chopped

5 ounces milk chocolate, finely chopped

6 ounces white chocolate, finely chopped

1½ cups heavy cream, chilled

1¼ teaspoons unflavored gelatin

1½ tablespoons cool water

1 tablespoon unsweetened cocoa powder

Making three different chocolate mousses may seem like a chore, but it's not that difficult and the result is well worth the effort. Be sure to chop the chocolate very fine so that it will melt on contact with the hot vanilla sauce.

1. Make the meringue layers: Position the oven racks in the bottom third and top third of the oven, and preheat the oven to 350 degrees. Line two baking sheets with parchment paper. With a dark pencil, trace two 10-inch circles on each of the pieces of parchment paper. Flip the paper over on the baking sheets so the pencil side is down.

2. In a large bowl, combine the hazelnut flour, ½ cup of the sugar, and the all-purpose flour. Stir in the milk. The mixture should have the consistency of mashed potatoes.

3. Place the egg whites in the bowl of an electric mixer fitted with the whisk attachment, and whip on high speed until just about to hold soft peaks. With the mixer still on high, pour in the remaining 1 cup sugar in a slow, steady stream. Whip until the meringue holds stiff peaks.

4. Fold half of the meringue into the hazelnut flour paste to lighten it. Then gently fold in the remaining meringue, being careful not to deflate it.

5. Fit a pastry bag with a #8 tip (or a tip measuring ¾ inch in diameter), and fill it with the meringue. Pipe the meringue into 10-inch rounds on the prepared baking sheets: Starting from the center of each circle and holding the pastry bag upright, pipe in a spiral motion, moving outward toward the border you have drawn. Sprinkle the chopped hazelnuts over the meringue rounds and dust with the confectioners' sugar.

6. Place the baking sheets in the oven and leave the oven door cracked open about ½ inch. Bake for 20 minutes, switching the positions of the baking sheets after 10 minutes. Then turn the temperature down to 300 degrees and bake until the meringue layers are firm and golden, about 40 minutes more, switching positions after 20 minutes.

7. Remove the meringues from the oven and slide them off the baking sheets onto wire racks, parchment-lined side down. Allow to cool completely. Use immediately, or leave the meringues on the parchment paper, drape them loosely with plastic wrap, and store at room temperature for up to 1 week.

8. When you are ready to assemble the cake, trim the meringue layers so that they will fit inside a 10-inch springform pan.

9. Place the Vanilla Sauce over a pot of lukewarm water, to keep it warm. Stir it occasionally as you work, but don't overheat it or it will curdle.

(cont. on next page)

10. Place the bittersweet, milk, and white chocolate in three separate 2-quart mixing bowls.

11. Mix ½ cup of the hot Vanilla Sauce into the bittersweet chocolate, and whisk until the chocolate is melted.

12. Whip ½ cup of the heavy cream until it holds stiff peaks. Whisk the bittersweet chocolate mixture into the whipped cream until the cream is streaked with chocolate; then continue to fold with a spatula until well combined.

13. Put 1 meringue layer inside the springform pan. Using a small offset spatula, spread the bittersweet chocolate mixture evenly over the meringue layer. Place another meringue layer on top, and place the pan in the freezer.

14. Mix ⅓ cup of the hot Vanilla Sauce into the milk chocolate. Whip ½ cup of heavy cream until it holds stiff peaks. Whisk the milk chocolate mixture into the whipped cream until the cream is streaked with chocolate; then continue to fold with a spatula until well combined.

15. Remove the pan from the freezer. Using a small offset spatula, spread the milk chocolate mixture over the meringue layer. Top with a third layer of meringue and return the pan to the freezer.

16. Combine the gelatin and the cool water in a small bowl, and stir to dissolve. Place 3 tablespoons of the hot Vanilla Sauce in a small bowl, and whisk in the gelatin mixture. Stir in the white chocolate. Cool to room temperature.

17. Whip the remaining ½ cup heavy cream until it holds stiff peaks. Whisk the white chocolate mixture into the whipped cream until smooth.

18. Remove the pan from the freezer. Using a small offset spatula, spread the white chocolate mixture over the meringue layer. Top with the fourth layer of meringue, making sure to place the flat side up. Cover the cake with plastic wrap and freeze it until firm, at least 2 hours (it will keep for up to 2 months).

19. To unmold the cake, heat a sharp paring knife over a gas burner or run it under very hot water and wipe it dry. Run the hot knife around the edge of the springform pan. Release the sides of the springform and transfer the cake to a serving platter.

20. Dust the top with the cocoa powder, and serve with the remaining Vanilla Sauce on the side.

Toasting Hazelnut Flour

To toast hazelnut flour, spread it out on a rimmed baking sheet and bake it in a preheated 400-degree oven, stirring it every 2 minutes so the flour near the edges of the sheet doesn't burn. Be sure to toast it well, until it is dark golden, about 6 minutes in all. When you remove the baking sheet from the oven, mound the flour in the center and let it cool—it will continue to toast a bit.

DACQUOISE with GANACHE

Serves 12

1 Classic Hazelnut Dacquoise (page 146), frozen for at least 2 hours and still in the pan (do not dust with cocoa powder)

1 cup Ganache (page 258)

1 tablespoon unsweetened cocoa powder

1 recipe Vanilla Sauce (page 251), optional

To decorate this cake, frost it with ganache that you pull into peaks, giving it a beautiful but homespun look. The ganache also adds more chocolatey richness to the cake. It's important to place the last layer of the meringue flat side up, so you'll have a smooth surface on which to spread the ganache. If you will be serving the cake soon after making it, rewarm the extra Vanilla Sauce and serve it on the side. If you will be storing the cake in the freezer for more than 3 days, make some fresh Vanilla Sauce before serving or simply skip the sauce and serve the cake as is.

1. Unmold the frozen cake: Heat a sharp paring knife over a gas burner or run it under very hot water and wipe it dry. Run the hot knife around the edge of the springform pan. Release the sides of the springform pan and transfer the cake to a serving platter.

2. Use a small offset spatula to spread a thin layer of ganache evenly over the top of the cake. Let it stand for 30 minutes to allow the ganache to set.

3. Spread the remaining ganache over the top of the cake with the spatula. Put a small amount of ganache on the tip of the spatula, and then tap the tip of the spatula over the entire surface of the cake, using an up-and-down motion, to pull peaks of ganache up from the surface.

4. Just before serving, dust the top of the cake with the cocoa powder. Serve the Vanilla Sauce on the side if desired.

Skinning Hazelnuts

To skin hazelnuts, place them on a rimmed baking sheet and bake them in a preheated 350-degree oven until fragrant, about 10 minutes. Wrap the hot nuts in a clean kitchen towel and set them aside for 10 to 15 minutes, to let the steam loosen the skins. Then rub the nuts with the towel to remove as much of the skin as possible.

MOONWALK CAKE

Serves 12

1 Classic Hazelnut Dacquoise
(page 146), frozen for at least
2 hours and still in the pan
(do not dust with cocoa
powder)

2 pounds Tempered Chocolate
(page 279)

1 cup Ganache (page 258)

1/2 cantaloupe

1/4 honeydew melon

10 large strawberries, washed,
stemmed, and allowed to
air-dry

8 kiwis, peeled

1/2 cup sugar

1 recipe Apricot Sauce (page
264)

I served this cake on several occasions when astronauts came to the White House. Chocolate molded onto a piece of bubble wrap creates a craterlike decoration for this cake, making it look like the surface of the moon (or what I imagine it to look like). Balls of colorful fruit provide a fanciful garnish. Use the very smallest size melon baller you can find to make the tiny "rocks." The crunchy chocolate on the outside is a wonderful contrast with the soft chocolate fillings. Two pounds of chocolate is generous for this recipe, but you don't want to run out. If you have leftover tempered chocolate, let it solidify in the bowl, and then wrap it in plastic wrap; it will keep indefinitely. Re-temper it along with some fresh chocolate next time.

1. Unmold the frozen cake: Heat a sharp paring knife over a gas burner or run it under very hot water and wipe it dry. Run the hot knife around the edge of the springform pan. Release the sides of the springform pan and transfer the cake to a serving platter.

2. Cut out a round of clean bubble wrap the same diameter as the cake. Cut a strip of bubble wrap that is the length of the perimeter of the cake and the width of the cake's sides. Place the two pieces of bubble wrap, bubble side up, on a work surface. Using a pastry brush, brush tempered chocolate all over the round of bubble wrap, covering it completely.

3. Use a small offset spatula to spread a thin layer of ganache evenly over the top of the cake. Before the tempered chocolate hardens, flip the round of bubble wrap on top of the cake, chocolate side down. Press evenly on the bubble wrap to make sure that the tempered chocolate adheres to the ganache.

4. Brush tempered chocolate onto the long strip of bubble wrap. While the chocolate is still soft, wrap the strip around the cake, chocolate side against the cake. Place the cake in the freezer for 20 to 30 minutes, to allow the chocolate to harden.

5. While the cake is in the freezer, use a very small melon baller to make balls of cantaloupe, honeydew, strawberries, and kiwi, reserving the leftover kiwi pieces.

6. Place the leftover kiwi pieces in a food processor and add the sugar. Process until just smooth (you don't want to puree the black seeds). Set aside in a small bowl.

7. At least 1 hour and up to 3 hours before serving, remove the cake from the freezer and peel away the bubble wrap. Place the balls of fruit randomly in the little craters on top of the cake. Just before serving, spoon the kiwi sauce and Apricot Sauce around the cake.

Chocolate Cakes at the White House

I probably made thirty or forty different chocolate cakes during my time at the White House, and they held an unusual place in my repertoire. For reasons I have trouble understanding, they were both loved and feared. Even though on average the chocolate cakes in this book have no more fat and calories than cakes made without chocolate, the ingredient sets off alarm bells for many health-conscious people. Every First Lady I worked for was wary of chocolate cakes to a certain degree. Most First Families absolutely loved chocolate but tended to restrict themselves to eating it on special occasions. George W. Bush had a favorite seven-layer chocolate cake that I'd make for him only on his birthday. The rest of the year he would try hard to abstain. Bill Clinton was allergic to chocolate and mostly avoided it, but he would sneak pieces of chocolate cake from the kitchen from time to time when no one was looking. I never told, because I was only the pastry chef, not his personal physician. Ronald Reagan was an absolute fiend for chocolate, but his wife watched his calories carefully and would allow only light, low-fat fresh fruit desserts to be served on a daily basis. When she was traveling, I would sometimes make some chocolate mousse for the President to enjoy secretly.

Now that nutritionists are discovering the benefits of chocolate, which contains heart-healthy flavonoids, maybe some of this fear will subside. I hope so, because in my opinion a beautiful chocolate cake should be a pure pleasure, not a guilty one, to be enjoyed by chocolate lovers any time dessert is served.

15. CHOCOLATE SOUFFLÉ CAKE

The difficulty with chocolate cake is getting a good chocolate flavor while avoiding a dense, heavy texture. This soufflé cake is feather-light but very chocolatey, making it one of my favorite chocolate cakes. I've always used inexpensive semisweet baking chocolate to make this particular cake. It contains less cocoa butter than more expensive chocolate, and when it bakes, its chocolate flavor comes through more powerfully because there is less fat to mute it. I leave out the egg yolks for the same reason. Yolks have their own strong flavor that fights with the chocolate, while whites offer structure without any taste.

CHOCOLATE-RASPBERRY ROULADE

Serves 16

6 ounces semisweet chocolate, finely chopped, or 6 ounces (1 cup) semisweet chocolate chips

8 large egg whites

3/4 cup sugar, plus more for sprinkling

6 tablespoons all-purpose flour

One 12-ounce jar seedless raspberry jam

1 recipe Vanilla Sauce (page 251)

2 cups fresh raspberries

This cake is simply filled with jam—no whipped cream or buttercream. It is lean, and the best way to really taste the chocolate in the cake.

1. Preheat the oven to 425 degrees. Line a 16 x 12-inch jelly roll pan with parchment paper.

2. Pour 2 inches of water into a small saucepan and bring it to a bare simmer. Place the chocolate in a stainless-steel bowl that is large enough to rest on top of the saucepan, and place it over the simmering water, making sure that the bowl doesn't touch the water. Heat, whisking occasionally, until the chocolate is completely melted. Set it aside to cool.

3. Place the egg whites in the bowl of an electric mixer fitted with the whisk attachment, and whip on high speed until just about to hold soft peaks. With the mixer still on high, pour in the sugar in a slow, steady stream. Whip until the whites hold stiff peaks. Turn the mixer to low speed and add the flour. When it has just been incorporated, turn the mixer to high speed and whip for 10 seconds. Fold in the cooled chocolate by hand, using a rubber spatula, taking care not to deflate the egg whites.

4. Fit a pastry bag with a ⅝-inch plain tip, and fill the bag with the batter. Starting in one corner, pipe back and forth the long way across the prepared jelly roll pan until about half the pan is covered with a 16 x 6-inch rectangle of batter. Bake until it is firm to the touch, 12 to 15 minutes. Place the pan on a wire rack and allow the cake to cool completely in the pan. (The cooled cake, still in the pan, can be wrapped in plastic wrap and kept at room temperature for up to 1 day, or frozen for up to 1 month.)

5. Sprinkle granulated sugar over a piece of parchment paper (to prevent sticking), and invert the cooled cake onto the paper. Peel off the other piece of parchment paper. Spread the raspberry jam over the cake.

6. Position the cake with a long edge facing you. Starting at the edge closest to you, fold over 1 inch of the cake. Slide a long ruler under the parchment, parallel to the folded edge. Use the ruler, pressed against the parchment and the cake, to help you roll the cake away from you into a tight roll. When the cake is rolled up, roll it back to the middle of the parchment and wrap the parchment tightly around it, twisting the ends of the paper to seal. Refrigerate until firm, about 20 minutes (or up to 2 days).

7. Place the chilled roulade on a serving platter and let it stand for about 20 minutes to come to room temperature. Just before serving, pour the Vanilla Sauce over the roulade and scatter the raspberries around it.

MOUSSE-FILLED CHOCOLATE SOUFFLÉ CAKE

Serves 16

FOR THE CARAMELIZED PECANS:

1 cup pecan halves

1/2 cup confectioners' sugar

1/2 vanilla bean, split lengthwise

FOR THE CAKE:

9 ounces semisweet chocolate, finely chopped, or 9 ounces (1 1/2 cups) semisweet chocolate chips

12 large egg whites

1 cup granulated sugar

1/2 cup all-purpose flour

FOR THE MOUSSE:

6 ounces semisweet or bittersweet chocolate, finely chopped

1 1/2 cups heavy cream, at room temperature

1 tablespoon finely chopped crystallized ginger

3/4 cup (6 ounces) seedless raspberry jam

Confectioners' sugar for dusting

Not completely happy with the desserts made by the part-time kitchen staff at Camp David, Mrs. Reagan asked me to start delivering desserts for special occasions there. This is one of the cakes that I often brought, because it travels very well. I remember one time when I had just finished decorating it and had stepped out of the kitchen for a breath of fresh air. Not ten steps away from me were President Reagan and Mikhail Gorbachev, strolling the grounds. I badly wanted to shake the Russian prime minister's hand, but they were so deep in conversation that they didn't notice me, and protocol wouldn't allow me to interrupt.

The pecans can be caramelized weeks in advance, but wait to make the simple mousse filling until just before you put the cake together, because it needs to be very soft and spreadable. I've made some of my most felicitous cake-decorating discoveries at the hardware store, including the stencil I use here to give the finished cake a beautiful confectioners' sugar design: I use a perforated aluminum sheet, which is used among other things as a screen for a radiator cover. They cost a pittance, can be cut to any size you need, and come in many pretty designs, including the one I have used for the last few years, which consists of tiny diamonds. Of course, you could always use a paper doily in a pinch!

1. Prepare the pecans: Combine the pecan halves and confectioners' sugar in a heavy saucepan. Using a sharp paring knife, scrape the seeds from the vanilla bean into the pan. Cook over medium-high heat, stirring constantly, until the sugar is completely dissolved and the syrup is light amber in color, 5 to 7 minutes.

2. Pour the coated nuts onto an ungreased sheet pan and allow them to cool completely. When they have hardened, chop them coarsely. (Caramelized pecans will keep in an airtight container at room temperature for up to 1 month.)

3. Make the cake: Preheat the oven to 425 degrees. Line a 16 x 12-inch jelly roll pan with parchment paper.

4. Pour 2 inches of water into a medium saucepan and bring it to a bare simmer. Place the chocolate in a stainless-steel bowl that is large enough to rest on top of the saucepan, and place it over the simmering water, making sure that the bowl doesn't touch the water. Heat, whisking occasionally, until the chocolate is completely melted. Set it aside to cool.

5. Place the egg whites in the bowl of an electric mixer fitted with the whisk attachment, and whip on high speed until just about to hold soft peaks. With the mixer still on high, pour in the sugar in a slow, steady stream. Whip until the whites hold stiff peaks. Turn the mixer to low speed and add the flour. When it has just been incorporated, turn the mixer to high speed and whip for 10 seconds. Then fold in the cooled chocolate by hand, using a rubber spatula, taking care not to deflate the egg whites.

(cont. on next page)

6. Fit a pastry bag with a ⅝-inch plain tip, and fill the bag with the batter. Starting in one corner, pipe back and forth the long way across the prepared pan until the pan is covered with batter. Bake until it is firm to the touch, 12 to 15 minutes. Place the pan on a wire rack and allow the cake to cool completely in the pan. (The cooled cake, still in the pan, can be wrapped in plastic wrap and kept at room temperature for up to 1 day or frozen for up to 1 month.)

7. Invert the cooled cake onto a cutting board, and peel off the parchment paper. Cut it crosswise into three pieces, and trim them if necessary so that each measures 5 x 12 inches.

8. Make the mousse: Pour 2 inches of water into a medium saucepan and bring to a bare simmer. Place the chocolate in a stainless-steel bowl that is large enough to rest on top of the saucepan, and place it over the simmering water, making sure that the bowl doesn't touch the water. Heat, whisking occasionally, until the chocolate is completely melted. Remove it from the heat and let it cool until the chocolate is just warm to the touch, between 95 and 100 degrees on an instant-read thermometer.

9. Whip the heavy cream with an electric mixer until it holds soft peaks. Add the whipped cream and the ginger to the chocolate all at once, and quickly whisk together.

10. Put the cake together: Place one cake strip on a cake board or a large serving platter. Spread half of the jam over the cake, reaching all the way to the edges. Spread half of the mousse over the jam, evenly and all the way to the edges. Sprinkle half of the pecans over the mousse. Repeat with the second cake layer, the remaining jam, all but 1 cup of the remaining mousse, and the remaining pecans. Place the third cake layer on top, with the flat side up. Smooth the remaining 1 cup of mousse over the top of the cake. Serve immediately or wrap the cake in plastic wrap and refrigerate it for up to 3 days before serving. (You can freeze it for up to 2 weeks; defrost it overnight in the refrigerator before serving.)

11. Place a perforated aluminum sheet on top of the cake and dust with confectioners' sugar. Carefully lift the sheet from the cake, and serve.

BÛCHE DE NOËL

Serves 16

6 ounces semisweet chocolate, finely chopped, or 6 ounces (1 cup) semisweet chocolate chips

8 large egg whites

¾ cup granulated sugar, plus extra for sprinkling

6 tablespoons all-purpose flour

One 12-ounce jar seedless raspberry jam

2 cups heavy cream

3 tablespoons confectioners' sugar

1 teaspoon pure vanilla extract

2 pints fresh raspberries

1 recipe Semisweet Chocolate Glaze (page 260)

Chocolate Bark (recipe follows)

1 Marzipan Squirrel (recipe follows)

Meringue Mushrooms (recipe follows)

1 recipe Raspberry Sauce (page 261)

No matter what their politics, all the First Families I served were very traditional when it came to holiday desserts. When Christmastime rolled around, I always made a Yule Log cake. Each family expressed delight in their own way. I remember one fall dinner, when President Reagan's daughter Maureen was visiting. It was always a pleasure to have Maureen Reagan at the White House, particularly at dinnertime, because she always brought her sense of humor. I brought a Yule Log to the table for the Reagans to enjoy, but also to evaluate as a possible dessert for an upcoming State Dinner for the German chancellor. Decorating the log, I pointed out, were two squirrels playing with their nuts. Maureen Reagan burst out laughing. I wanted the earth to swallow me whole, I was so embarrassed! But I got raves for the cake and the go-ahead for the State Dinner, so I guess my poor choice of words didn't ruin the dessert for them.

1. Preheat the oven to 425 degrees. Line a 16 x 12-inch jelly roll pan with parchment paper.

2. Pour 2 inches of water into a small saucepan and bring it to a bare simmer. Place the chocolate in a stainless-steel bowl that is large enough to rest on top of the saucepan, and place it over the simmering water, making sure that the bowl doesn't touch the water. Heat, whisking occasionally, until the chocolate is completely melted. Set it aside to cool.

3. Place the egg whites in the bowl of an electric mixer fitted with the whisk attachment, and whip on high speed until just about to hold soft peaks. With the mixer still on high, pour in the sugar in a slow, steady stream. Whip until the whites hold stiff peaks. Turn the mixer to low speed and add the flour. When it has just been incorporated, turn the mixer to high speed and whip for 10 seconds. Fold in the cooled chocolate by hand, using a rubber spatula, taking care not to deflate the egg whites.

4. Fit a pastry bag with a ⅝-inch plain tip, and fill the bag with the batter. Starting in one corner, pipe back and forth the short way across the prepared jelly roll pan until about half the pan is covered with a 12 x 12-inch square of batter. Bake until it is firm to the touch, 12 to 15 minutes. Place the pan on a wire rack and allow the cake to cool completely in the pan. (The cooled cake, still in the pan, can be wrapped in plastic wrap and kept at room temperature for up to 1 day, or frozen for up to 1 month.)

5. Sprinkle granulated sugar over a piece of parchment paper (to prevent sticking), and invert the cooled cake onto the paper. Peel off the other piece of parchment paper. Spread the raspberry jam over the cake.

(cont. on next page)

6. Place the cream in the bowl of an electric mixer fitted with the whisk attachment, and whip on high speed until soft peaks appear. Add the confectioners' sugar and vanilla, and continue to whip until the cream just holds stiff peaks. Do not overwhip. Spread the whipped cream on top of the jam. Arrange the raspberries on top of the whipped cream, pressing down on them slightly to embed them in the cream.

7. Starting at the edge closest to you, fold over 1 inch of the cake. Slide a long ruler under the parchment, parallel to the folded edge. Use the ruler, pressed against the parchment and the cake, to help you roll the cake away from you into a tight roll. When the cake is rolled up, roll it back to the middle of the parchment and wrap the parchment tightly around it, twisting the ends of the paper to seal. Refrigerate until firm, about 1 hour (or up to 1 day).

8. Remove the parchment from the log and place it, seam side down, on a serving platter. Lightly paint the surface of the cake with the Semisweet Chocolate Glaze. Place the Chocolate Bark on top of the glaze so it adheres to the cake. Set the Marzipan Squirrel on the log, or next to it, and arrange the mushrooms around the log. Just before serving, pour the Raspberry Sauce all around the log. (If you like, you can refrigerate the bûche, uncovered, for up to 3 hours before serving. Let it stand for about 20 minutes to come to room temperature. Do not add the Raspberry Sauce until you are ready to serve it.)

Marzipan Squirrel

Makes 1 squirrel

Brown food coloring

2¼ ounces marzipan

1 large egg white

1 piece dry spaghetti

Royal icing

Dark chocolate icing

To make a marzipan squirrel to decorate the Bûche de Noël, follow these simple directions, consulting the photograph in the insert as you work.

1. Knead some brown food coloring into the marzipan to color it a squirrel-brown. Roll a 1-ounce piece into a ball; this will be the body. Roll two ½-ounce pieces into balls; these will be the head and the tail. Roll two tiny pieces of marzipan into tiny balls; these will be the ears.

2. Roll the larger ball into an egg shape, and then make a ¼-inch cut into each side of the narrow end of the egg, discarding the triangles of marzipan, to form the two front legs. Use a paring knife to form the haunches and back legs on either side of the wide end of the egg. Then use the paring knife to create the paws at the end of each leg.

3. Press and roll a smaller ball into a feather shape for the tail. Attach the tail to the body with a little egg white. Insert a small piece of spaghetti through the underside of the tail and into the body so it will stay in place.

4. Roll the remaining small ball into an olive shape for the head. Attach it to the body, using a little egg white, and secure it with another small piece of spaghetti.

5. Flatten the two tiny balls into pointy ear shapes and glue them to the head with egg white.

6. To make the eyes: Let the squirrel dry for 24 hours, then pipe large dots of royal icing onto the head, and then smaller dots of dark chocolate onto the larger white dots.

Meringue Mushrooms

**Makes about
24 mushrooms**

1 cup granulated sugar

1 cup confectioners' sugar

1½ tablespoons all-purpose flour

4 large egg whites, at room temperature

Unsweetened cocoa powder for dusting

These meringue mushrooms decorate the Bûche de Noël. Serve the extras as crunchy cookies during the holidays.

1. Position the oven racks in the top and bottom thirds of the oven, and preheat the oven to 275 degrees. Line two baking sheets with parchment paper, and set them aside.

2. Sift ½ cup of the granulated sugar, the confectioners' sugar, and the flour together into a bowl. Place the egg whites in the bowl of an electric mixer fitted with the whisk attachment, and whip on high speed until just about to hold soft peaks. With the mixer still on high, slowly pour in the remaining ½ cup granulated sugar in a slow, steady stream. Whip until the meringue holds stiff peaks. Then fold in the flour mixture by hand, using a rubber spatula, taking care not to deflate the meringue.

3. Fit a pastry bag with a large plain tip, and fill it with the meringue. Pipe stem shapes onto the prepared baking sheets by holding the bag perpendicular to the baking sheet, squeezing, and pulling up about 1 inch. Release the bag before pulling the tip away from the meringue.

4. Bake the stems until they are partially dry, 30 to 40 minutes.

5. Line the remaining baking sheet with a damp kitchen towel, and cover the towel with a sheet of parchment, dabbing a little meringue on the underside corners of the parchment to fix it to the towel. (The towel will keep the bottoms of the mushroom caps moist and sticky and the insides chewy rather than hard.)

6. Pipe the mushroom caps onto the parchment by holding the bag perpendicular to the baking sheet and squeezing out buttons about 1 inch in diameter. Dust them with cocoa powder, and bake for 30 minutes, so they are still soft on the inside.

7. As soon as they are hard enough to be picked up, stick the caps on the cooled stems (work quickly because the tops will still be sticky). Place the mushrooms, upright, on the baking sheet.

8. Lower the oven temperature to 200 degrees and bake until the meringue mushrooms are dry, 2 hours. They will keep in an airtight container at room temperature for up to 1 month.

Chocolate Bark

1 pound tempered white or milk chocolate (page 279)

1 pound tempered dark chocolate (page 279)

To simulate wood bark in chocolate, I use a rubber wood-graining tool that's sold at art supply and hardware stores and sometimes at wallpaper stores. They're inexpensive and easy to find. It's too difficult to temper less than a pound of chocolate at a time, so this recipe calls for a pound of each. You can make just enough bark to cover the cake (judge this by eye) and let the remaining chocolate solidify, to temper again another time. Or make extra bark—you can use it to decorate many other cakes and pastries. Save leftovers in an airtight container for up to 2 months.

1. Line a baking sheet with parchment paper. Dampen a countertop by running a clean, moist sponge or kitchen towel over it. Place an 18-inch-long sheet of plastic wrap on top of the damp counter (the water will make it stick, so it won't move while you are working).

2. Dip your wood-graining tool into the white or milk chocolate, and drag the tool across the plastic wrap with a rocking motion, covering the area with a thin layer of chocolate in a wood-grain pattern. Repeat, covering the entire piece of plastic wrap with wood-grain chocolate.

(cont. on next page)

Let it cool completely, about 5 minutes.

3. When the wood-grain chocolate has cooled, spread a thin layer of dark chocolate over it, using a small offset spatula. As soon as the chocolate begins to set up, but before it has completely hardened, use a sharp paring knife or scissors to cut the sheet of chocolate, still attached to the plastic wrap, into uneven pieces, 2 or 3 inches long and about 1½ inches wide, bending them so that they'll fit on the surface of the log. Place the chocolate pieces on the parchment-lined baking sheet and refrigerate until firm, 20 to 30 minutes.

4. Peel the plastic away from the chocolate pieces just before placing them on the log, arranging them to look like bark.

16. PRESIDENT AND MRS. CARTER'S DOME CAKE

When I arrived at the White House during the last year of the Carter administration, I was awed by my new responsibilities and terrified about making a mistake. People probably thought I was not very friendly because I was so absorbed in my work that I hardly spoke to anyone. One person I did speak to was the previous pastry chef, Albert Kumin, who had been at my job interview and stayed on for the first few days to acquaint me with the kitchen. I was anxious to learn what kinds of desserts the Carter family had enjoyed in the past. One of their favorites, he said, was a very dense, rich chocolate dome cake.

When I got the job, I had promised Mrs. Carter that I was going to make desserts on the lighter side, so I decided to re-create the Chocolate Dome Cake my way. It's probably not lower in calories than the cake they had been eating previously, but it has a lighter feel to it. The cake layers are made with biscuit macaroon, a very fluffy, soft cake that I stumbled upon one day when I accidentally doubled the egg whites in a regular macaroon recipe; the result was a puffy, cakelike cookie that I thought would be delicious layered with a mousse. Instead of a dark chocolate mousse, I decided to layer my cake with white chocolate mousse, which is lighter on the palate. The Carters loved this new version as much as the old, and I began to relax and really enjoy my job and the people around me.

CHOCOLATE DOME with GRAND MARNIER MOUSSE

Serves 12

FOR THE CHOCOLATE BISCUIT MACAROON:

3 tablespoons whole milk, plus more if necessary

1 cups almond flour

³/₄ cups sugar

2 tablespoons all-purpose flour

3 tablespoons unsweetened cocoa powder

6 large egg whites

FOR THE WHITE CHOCOLATE–ORANGE MOUSSE:

9 ounces best-quality white chocolate

1 cup heavy cream, at room temperature

¹/₂ cup Grand Marnier or other orange-flavored liqueur

¹/₂ cup coarsely chopped unsalted pistachio nuts

TO FINISH:

White Chocolate Curls (page 278)

Here's my Dome Cake in its basic version: layers of chocolate biscuit macaroon sandwiched together with a rich white chocolate–orange mousse.

If you have leftover batter after piping the cake rounds onto the parchment, line another baking sheet with parchment paper and pipe the remaining batter in quarter-size rounds. Bake the cookies for 15 to 20 minutes in a 350-degree oven, and when they are cool, sandwich them together with a dab of your favorite jam and dust them with confectioners' sugar. Here's how French pastry chefs remove their macaroons easily from the parchment: Carefully lift up a corner of the paper and pour a little bit of water onto the baking sheet, being careful not to get the cookies wet. The cookies will pop right off the paper.

1. Make the biscuit macaroon layers: Position oven racks in the top and bottom thirds of the oven, and preheat the oven to 350 degrees. Line a 5-cup stainless-steel bowl with two layers of plastic wrap, making sure that at least 1 inch of plastic overhangs the bowl on all sides; set it aside. Line two baking sheets with parchment paper. Use a dark pencil to draw 5 circles on the parchment: one measuring 3¹/₂ inches in diameter, one measuring 5 inches in diameter, two measuring 6 inches in diameter, and one measuring 7¹/₂ inches in diameter. Flip the parchment over so that the pencil markings are on the underside but still visible.

Unsweetened cocoa powder
for dusting

1 recipe Raspberry Sauce
(page 261)

2. Combine the milk, the almond flour, ½ cup of the sugar, the all-purpose flour, and the cocoa powder in a large bowl. Stir to make a soft paste. If the mixture is too dry, stir in more milk, 1 teaspoon at a time, until it has the consistency of stiff mashed potatoes.

3. Place the egg whites in the bowl of an electric mixer fitted with the whisk attachment, and whip on high speed until just about to hold soft peaks. With the mixer still on high, pour in the remaining 1 cup sugar in a slow, steady stream. Whip until the meringue holds stiff peaks.

4. Fold the cocoa mixture into the meringue in two separate additions, being careful not to deflate it. Scrape the batter into a pastry bag fitted with a plain #6 or #7 tip. Starting in the center of one of the circles you drew, holding the pastry bag upright, pipe in a spiral motion, moving outward toward the border. Repeat with the remaining circles. Place the baking sheet in the oven and leave the oven door cracked open 1 inch. Bake for 20 minutes. Then turn the temperature down to 300 degrees and bake until the meringue rounds are firm and golden, about 40 minutes more. Allow to cool completely on the baking sheets.

(cont. on next page)

5. Make the mousse: Pour 2 inches of water into a medium saucepan and bring to a bare simmer. Place the chocolate in a stainless-steel bowl that is large enough to rest on top of the saucepan, and place it over the simmering water, making sure that the bowl doesn't touch the water. Heat, whisking occasionally, until the chocolate is completely melted. Remove from the heat and let cool until the chocolate is just warm to touch, between 95 and 100 degrees on an instant-read thermometer.

6. Whip the heavy cream with an electric mixer until it holds soft peaks. Gently but quickly fold the whipped cream, Grand Marnier, and pistachios into the melted chocolate, adding them all at once.

7. Scrape the mousse into a pastry bag fitted with a #6 or #7 plain tip. Starting at the bottom center of the plastic wrap–lined bowl, pipe in a spiral motion, moving outward and upward toward the top of the bowl, creating a ⅓-inch-thick layer of mousse covering the inside of the bowl. Place the 3½-inch macaroon round in the bottom of the bowl, laying it flat on the layer of mousse. Make sure that it fits snugly but does not poke through the mousse to the sides of the bowl (you don't want to see any cake layers when you unmold the dessert). If it is too big, trim it a little bit all around so it is the right size. Repeat with the other rounds, going from smallest to largest and trimming as necessary, pressing on each meringue layer as you fit it in so the dessert will be compacted. Wrap tightly in plastic wrap and freeze for at least 1 hour (or up to 2 weeks).

8. To unmold the cake, remove the plastic wrap from the top of the bowl. Invert a serving platter over the bowl, and invert. Gently tug on the plastic lining, lifting away the bowl. Peel the plastic away from the cake. If the cake is very hard, let it stand on the counter for 30 minutes to soften up.

9. Just before serving, sprinkle the dome with White Chocolate Curls and then lightly dust it with cocoa powder so you can still see the white chocolate. Slice, and serve with the Raspberry Sauce on the side.

RASPBERRY-GLAZED CHOCOLATE DOME CAKE

Serves 12

½ cup cold water

½ envelope unflavored gelatin

1½ cups Raspberry Sauce (page 261), at room temperature

1 Chocolate Dome with Grand Marnier Mousse (page 170), frozen for at least 1 hour, still in the mold

1 recipe Sweetened Whipped Cream (page 248)

The white of the whipped cream and the deep red of the glaze on this cake make a striking combination. Let the cake come to room temperature before serving; about 30 minutes on the counter should do it.

1. Pour 1 inch of water into a small saucepan and bring it to a bare simmer. Place the cold water in a small heatproof bowl and sprinkle the gelatin on top. Let stand to dissolve. Then place the bowl on top of the simmering water and heat, whisking constantly, just until the gelatin melts, 30 seconds to 1 minute. Whisk the melted gelatin into the Raspberry Sauce. Set it aside until it has thickened slightly, 30 minutes. Don't let it become too thick to pour.

2. Unmold the cake: Remove the plastic wrap from the top of the bowl. Place a cardboard cake round the same diameter as the cake on top of the bowl, and invert. Gently tug on the plastic lining, lifting away the bowl. Peel the plastic away from the cake.

3. Place the cake on a wire rack set over a rimmed baking sheet. Pour the raspberry glaze over the cake, covering it completely. Put the cake in the freezer to firm up the glaze, 10 minutes.

4. Transfer the glazed cake to a serving platter. Pour any remaining glaze around the cake (if it has thickened too much to pour, reheat it for a few seconds in the microwave).

5. Scrape the Sweetened Whipped Cream into a pastry bag fitted with a #4 or #5 star tip. Pipe a border around the base of the dome. Pipe a few rosettes on the top of the dome. Let stand 30 minutes before serving.

RUBIES and GOLD DOME CAKE

Serves 12

1 Chocolate Dome with Grand Marnier Mousse (page 170), frozen for at least 1 hour, still in the mold

2 pints fresh raspberries

2 pints golden raspberries, cantaloupe balls, or blackberries

½ cup semisweet chocolate chips

1 recipe Lemon Cream (page 250)

1 recipe Raspberry Sauce (page 261)

The straight lines of beautifully colored fruit on this cake make a simple but impressive decoration. I call it Rubies and Gold when I use alternating rows of red and gold raspberries. If you can't find the golden berries, make small cantaloupe balls, about the size of raspberries, instead. Or use blackberries and call it "Rubies and Sapphires." With this cake I recommend a Gewürztraminer wine, which is a fruity, sweet wine that goes well with the fruit and white chocolate.

1. Unmold the cake: Remove the plastic wrap from the top of the bowl. Invert a flat serving platter, at least 16 inches in diameter, on top of the bowl, and invert. Gently tug on the plastic lining, lifting away the bowl. Peel the plastic away from the cake. Let the cake stand on the counter until the mousse has softened, about 30 minutes.

2. Starting at the base of the cake, arrange some of the red raspberries close together all around it, pressing them into the mousse so they'll adhere. Arrange a row of golden raspberries above the red raspberries in the same way. Continue until the cake is completely covered and you've reached the top. You should have four or five rows of each kind of berry.

3. Place the chocolate chips in a microwave-safe bowl and heat until melted and just warm. (Or melt the chocolate in the top of a double boiler.) Stir in a few drops of water, to thicken the chocolate to the consistency of buttercream (be careful not to add too much water, or your chocolate will get too stiff). Scrape the chocolate into a pastry bag fitted with the smallest plain tip you have. Pipe a ring of semicircles, each about 2 inches long and 1½ inches wide, all around the base of the cake (see photo insert). You should have 15 or 16 when you are through.

4. Spoon some Lemon Cream inside each chocolate semicircle. Cover the rest of the platter with the Raspberry Sauce. Serve immediately, or let stand for up to 3 hours before serving.

17. PRINCESS MARY CAKE

In 1976 I became one in the long line of pastry chefs at the Homestead Hotel in Hot Springs, Virginia. This cake was already on the menu when I arrived, and had been for many years. It was part of the tradition at this grande dame of great American resort hotels. I don't know who Princess Mary was, but I imagine that this cake was so named because of its rich, velvety, royal quality. It is absolutely delightful and I can picture the Queen of England enjoying it with a cup of tea.

PRINCESS MARY CAKE with CHESTNUT CREAM and GANACHE FROSTING

Serves 16

FOR THE CAKE:

6 tablespoons all-purpose flour

6 tablespoons cornstarch

1 teaspoon baking powder

6 ounces (1 cup) semisweet chocolate chips

½ cup (1 stick) unsalted butter, softened

½ cup plus 2 tablespoons granulated sugar

4 large eggs, separated, at room temperature

---

1 cup (2 sticks) unsalted butter, softened

4 tablespoons dark rum

One 17-ounce can sweet chestnut spread, preferably Clement Faugier

Confectioners' sugar, if necessary

4 cups Ganache made with semisweet chocolate chips (page 258), cooled

⅔ cup Light Syrup (page 264)

Chestnut spread can be found in specialty foods stores and online. I use the Clement Faugier brand, which is widely available and I think the best (see Resources, page 283). It comes sweetened, but some brands are sweeter than others, so taste your chestnut cream and if it isn't sweet enough, beat in some confectioners' sugar to taste. Make the ganache with semisweet chocolate chips. Their relatively low cocoa butter content will ensure that the ganache doesn't separate and is easy to whip and reheat as a beautiful, shiny glaze.

1. Make the cake: Preheat the oven to 375 degrees. Grease a 9 x 2-inch-deep round cake pan. Line the bottom of the pan with parchment paper, dust it with flour, and tap out any excess.

2. Sift the flour, cornstarch, and baking powder together into a small bowl. Set aside.

3. Pour 2 inches of water into a small saucepan and bring to a bare simmer. Place the chocolate chips in a stainless-steel bowl that is large enough to rest on top of the saucepan, and place it on top of the simmering water, making sure that the bowl doesn't touch the water. Heat, whisking occasionally, until the chocolate is completely melted. Set it aside to cool.

4. Combine the butter and the ½ cup sugar in the bowl of an electric mixer fitted with the paddle attachment. Cream on medium-high speed until smooth but not fluffy, about 3 minutes. Do not overmix. Add the egg yolks, one at a time, scraping down the sides of the bowl after each addition. Stir in the chocolate. Stir in the flour mixture. The mixture should resemble chocolate buttercream.

5. Place the egg whites in a clean bowl and fit the mixer with the whisk attachment. Whip on high speed until just about to hold soft peaks. With the mixer still on high, pour in the remaining 2 tablespoons granulated sugar in a slow, steady stream. Whip until the whites hold stiff peaks.

6. Using a rubber spatula, fold half of the egg whites into the chocolate batter; then fold in the remaining half. At this point, the batter will look like chocolate mousse. Pour the batter into the prepared pan and bake until a toothpick inserted in the center comes out clean, 35 to 45 minutes. Let the cake rest in the pan on a wire rack for 5 minutes. Then invert the cake onto a wire rack, invert it again so it is right side up, and let it cool completely on the wire rack. (The cake can be wrapped in plastic wrap and then in foil and frozen for up to 1 month. Defrost overnight in the refrigerator before using.)

(cont. on next page)

7. Make the chestnut cream: Place the soft butter in the bowl of an electric mixer fitted with the paddle attachment. Beat on medium-high speed until light and fluffy, about 1 minute, scraping down the sides of the bowl once or twice as necessary. Beat in 2 tablespoons of the rum. Add the chestnut spread and beat until smooth, scraping down the sides of the bowl once or twice as necessary. Taste, and beat in some confectioners' sugar if the mixture is not sweet enough. Set the chestnut cream aside.

8. Scrape half of the ganache into a bowl and set it aside. Whip the other half of the ganache until it is fluffy, lightened, and the consistency of buttercream. Scrape this into a pastry bag fitted with a #4 plain tip.

9. Combine the Light Syrup and the remaining 2 tablespoons rum in a small bowl.

10. Using a sharp serrated knife, slice the cake horizontally into three equal layers. Place the bottom layer on a 9-inch cardboard cake round. Spread about ⅔ cup of the chestnut cream in an even layer over the top. Pipe a round of ganache, about 2 inches in diameter, in the center of the cake. Pipe a ring around the round, leaving a space of about 1¾ inches in between. Pipe another ring right at the edge of the cake.

11. Place the second cake layer on top, and push down slightly so the layers adhere. Brush the top of the layer with half of the rum syrup. Repeat the frosting of chestnut cream and the rings of ganache, as described above. Place the third layer on top, press it down lightly, and brush with the remaining rum syrup. Refrigerate the cake for 30 minutes.

12. Heat the reserved bowl of ganache in a microwave or above a pot of simmering water until it is warm and pourable. Stir it gently so you don't create any air bubbles in it.

13. Place the chilled cake on a wire rack set over a rimmed baking sheet. Slowly pour the warm ganache over the cake, using a small offset spatula to smooth it evenly over the top. Gently tap the rack so that the ganache runs down the sides of the cake, and smooth it with the spatula where necessary in order to cover the cake completely. Use a large metal spatula to transfer the cake to a serving platter. (Scrape the leftover ganache into an airtight container and refrigerate it, reserving it for another use.) Serve the cake immediately or let it stand at room temperature, covered with a cake dome, for up to 1 day.

14. To slice the cake, use a sharp chef's knife or a serrated knife, rinsing it in hot water and drying it with a clean paper towel after every slice, so that you don't smear the ganache over each piece of cake.

PRINCESS MARY CAKE with RASPBERRY FLOWERS

Serves 16

1 Princess Mary Cake with Chestnut Cream and Ganache Frosting (page 180)

16 large raspberries

1 recipe American Buttercream (page 256), colored light green

Princess Mary Cake is easily transformed into a colorful special-occasion dessert. Here the leftover ganache is whipped to a buttercream-like consistency and piped around the cake. Large raspberries become the flowers at the center of the ganache rosettes. The leaves are made from a very simple American-style buttercream, perfect for this use.

1. Transfer the glazed cake to a serving platter and scrape the leftover ganache into a mixing bowl. Whip the ganache with an electric mixer until it is lightened in color and the consistency of buttercream. Scrape it into a pastry bag fitted with a #6 star tip. Pipe rosettes of the ganache around the top edge of the cake. You should have about 16 rosettes. Place a raspberry in the center of each rosette.

2. Scrape the American Buttercream into a pastry bag fitted with a leaf tip. Pipe a green buttercream leaf at the base of each raspberry. Serve the cake immediately, or hold it at room temperature, covered with a cake dome, for up to 1 day.

3. To slice the cake, use a sharp chef's knife or a serrated knife, rinsing it in hot water and drying it with a clean paper towel after every slice so you don't smear the ganache over each piece of cake.

PRINCESS MARY CAKE with ROYAL CROWN and MADEIRA SABAYON

Serves 16

FOR THE NOUGAT CROWN:

1½ cups sugar

½ vanilla bean, split lengthwise

1½ cups sliced almonds

FOR THE MADEIRA SABAYON:

4 large egg yolks

½ cup sugar

3½ tablespoons Madeira

2¾ cups heavy cream

1 Princess Mary Cake with Chestnut Cream and Ganache Frosting (page 180)

1 recipe American Buttercream (page 256), divided into 4 portions and colored pink, red, yellow, and green

The addition of a beautiful caramel crown makes this a truly regal cake. Don't discard the leftover nougat—you can crush it and sprinkle it over the sabayon.

1. Make the nougat crown: Preheat the oven to 250 degrees. Line a rimmed baking sheet with a Silpat and have another Silpat at the ready.

2. Place the sugar in a heavy saucepan. Use a sharp paring knife to scrape the seeds from the vanilla bean into the pan. (Reserve the bean for another use.) Cook over medium-high heat, stirring constantly, until the sugar melts and becomes a uniform amber color, 5 to 7 minutes.

3. Stir in the sliced almonds, and pour the nougat onto the Silpat-lined baking sheet. Top with the second Silpat, and use a rolling pin to roll the nougat into as thin a layer as possible (it should be at least 12 inches across). If the nougat hardens too quickly, put the baking sheet in the oven for 2 or 3 minutes to soften it up, and then continue to roll.

(cont. on next page)

4. Peel away the top Silpat. Place a 9-inch cake pan on top of the nougat and use a heavy chef's knife to cut around it, forming a 9-inch round of nougat. If the nougat has gotten too hard and brittle to cut, put the baking sheet back in the oven for another 2 to 3 minutes to soften it, and then proceed. Cut the round in half and then into quarters. Cut each quarter into thirds. If at any point the nougat gets too hard to work with, reheat it again in the oven before proceeding.

5. Keep the nougat triangles warm and pliable by working near the open oven door. Pick up each triangle and bend the pointy tip back, making sure all the tips are bending the same way. Set the bent triangles on a piece of parchment paper to cool and harden. (If you are not satisfied with the looks of any of the triangles, they can be reshaped after rewarming them on the baking sheet in the oven.)

6. Make the Madeira Sabayon: Pour 2 inches of water into a large saucepan and bring to a bare simmer. Combine the egg yolks, sugar, and Madeira in a bowl that is large enough to fit on top of the saucepan, and place it over the simmering water. Whisk until the mixture is very pale, has increased in volume, and is hot to the touch (120 degrees on an instant-read thermometer). Remove the bowl from the heat and whip the mixture with an electric mixer on high speed until it is fluffy and has cooled to warm room temperature.

7. In another bowl, whip the heavy cream until it just holds soft peaks. Fold it into the sabayon. Cover with plastic wrap and refrigerate for at least 1 hour and up to 3 hours before using.

8. Transfer the glazed cake to a serving platter. Position the nougat triangles around the top edge of the cake with the wide end down and the bent tips pointing up and out, so that they resemble a golden crown (see photo insert).

9. Fit a pastry bag with a petal tip, and pipe little pink, red, and yellow buttercream roses, in groups of three, at the base of each piece of nougat (using a new bag for each color). Use the green buttercream and a leaf tip to pipe a few little leaves.

10. Slice, and serve with the Madeira Sabayon on the side.

18. MRS. CLINTON'S COFFEE GENOISE

Mrs. Clinton loved coffee desserts in every form. The Mocha Cake in my book *Dessert University* was a favorite. Espresso sorbet, served with cinnamon whipped cream, was another. I turned to this recipe for Coffee Genoise again and again because it is so versatile, and because the genoise, flavored with instant espresso powder, takes on a strong, pure coffee flavor.

SIMPLE COFFEE GENOISE

Serves 8

FOR THE CAKE:

1 tablespoon instant espresso powder

1 tablespoon hot water

4 large eggs

1/2 cup plus 1 tablespoon sugar

1 cup all-purpose flour, sifted

Pinch salt

4 tablespoons unsalted butter, melted and cooled

TO FINISH:

1 recipe cinnamon-flavored Sweetened Whipped Cream (page 248)

1 cup finely chopped walnuts

I was able to put this simple version together in about an hour—perfect for those times when something warm from the oven was needed in a hurry.

1. Combine the espresso powder and hot water in a small bowl and stir to dissolve. Set aside to cool.

2. Preheat the oven to 375 degrees. Grease a 9 x 2-inch-deep round cake pan. Line the bottom of the pan with parchment paper and grease the paper. Dust the pan with flour, and tap out any excess.

3. Pour 2 inches of water into a medium saucepan, and bring to a bare simmer. Combine the eggs and sugar in the bowl of an electric mixer fitted with the whisk attachment. Place the bowl over the simmering water and whisk constantly, by hand or with a handheld mixer, until the egg mixture is just lukewarm to the touch, 86 to 90 degrees on an instant-read thermometer.

4. Return the bowl to the mixer and whisk on high speed for 5 minutes. Then reduce the speed to medium and whisk until the mixture is completely cool, thick, and shiny, another 12 minutes.

5. Using a rubber spatula, fold in the flour, salt, and espresso mixture. Spoon about 1 cup of the batter into a small mixing bowl and stir in the butter; then carefully fold the batter-and-butter mixture back into the larger bowl of batter.

6. Pour the batter into the prepared pan and bake until a toothpick inserted into the center comes out clean, about 30 minutes more.

7. Remove the pan from the oven and immediately turn the cake out onto a cake plate or serving platter. (The cooled cake can be wrapped in plastic wrap and frozen for up to 2 weeks; defrost it on the counter.) Let the cake cool slightly, and then slice it, topping each slice with a dollop of cinnamon whipped cream and a tablespoon of chopped walnuts.

CHOCOLATE MOUSSE-COVERED COFFEE GENOISE

Serves 10

1 Simple Coffee Genoise (page 190), cooled

1 recipe Quick Chocolate Mousse (page 259), freshly made and spreadable

Chocolate Curls (page 278)

This pretty cake is simpler to make than it would appear. The chocolate mousse is just a combination of whipped cream and melted chocolate. The decorations—chocolate curls—are easy to accomplish although impressive to look at, and they also cover up any bumps and imperfections that appear in the frosting. If I had a frozen Coffee Genoise on hand, I was able to put this dessert together in about 15 minutes—which came in very handy during President Clinton's tenure, when there was often a sudden desperate need for dessert at whatever hour of the day or night.

1. Place the genoise on a serving platter. Slide strips of parchment paper underneath the cake so that about 2 inches all around the cake is covered with paper.

2. Coat the sides of the cake with some of the mousse. Spread more of the mousse on top, covering the top evenly.

3. Carefully slide the paper strips out from under the cake, and discard them.

4. Just before serving, mound some Chocolate Curls on top of the cake and scatter some around the sides of the cake.

5. Serve immediately, or refrigerate (uncovered) for up to 6 hours and let come to room temperature before serving.

COFFEE GENOISE with MOCHA BUTTERCREAM

Serves 12

½ cup hot, strong brewed coffee

2 tablespoons sugar

2 tablespoons Kahlúa or other coffee-flavored liqueur

1 Simple Coffee Genoise (page 190), cooled

1 recipe English Custard Coffee Buttercream (page 257)

1 cup finely chopped walnuts

The buttercream that I use here, a coffee-flavored English custard style, is particularly rich and delicious. The technique is a little more involved than the method for making American buttercream frosting, but it is well worth the effort. This cake was Mrs. Clinton's absolute favorite, one she requested over and over again, both for special occasions and also as an occasional indulgence for no reason at all.

1. Combine the hot coffee, sugar, and Kahlúa in a small bowl and set aside to cool.

2. Using a sharp, serrated knife, slice the genoise horizontally into three equal layers. Place 1 layer on a cardboard cake round and sprinkle it with some of the coffee syrup. Spread 1 cup of the buttercream evenly over the layer. Sprinkle ½ cup of the chopped nuts evenly over the buttercream. Place the second layer on top and repeat, sprinkling the layer with syrup, spreading with buttercream, and sprinkling with nuts. Place the third layer on top and repeat again, sprinkling the layer with syrup, spreading with buttercream, and sprinkling with nuts. Spread ½ cup of the buttercream around the sides of the cake. Refrigerate until the buttercream is firm, about 1 hour.

3. To finish, smooth 1 cup of the buttercream over the top and sides of the cake. Place the cake on a serving platter. Place the remaining buttercream in a pastry bag fitted with a small star tip, and pipe stars around the bottom and top edges of the cake. Serve immediately, or refrigerate (uncovered) for up to 1 day.

Puff Pastry and Choux Puff Cakes

akes made with puff pastry and choux puffs are common in France, but less so in the United States. That's too bad, because they are a nice change from the usual sponge cakes and butter cakes that commonly are served at birthday, anniversary, and wedding celebrations here. If you learn to make and use puff pastry and choux paste, not only will you be able to expand your cake repertoire to include French cake classics such as the Paris Brest and the croquembouche, but you will be able to use your newly acquired skills to make many other sweet and savory pastries, such as tarts, turnovers, napoleons, gougères, and éclairs.

19. HOLLANDER CAKE

I first learned to make this cake as a young pastry cook in Germany, where cakes with whipped cream are beloved. Its name probably indicates that it was originally made in Holland, but it was so popular in Hamburg, where I was living, that I have always considered it a truly German dessert. What I like best about it is the three different textures—the crunchy puff pastry, the smooth whipped cream, and the firm but yielding cherries. A little red currant jelly adds acidity, so the cake is not too sweet. It's interesting that everywhere I've worked, from the Georges V in Paris to the Savoy in London to the Homestead in Virginia to the White House, Hollander Cake was a favorite of the executive chef, who without fail would ask me to make it for him to serve at his own private dinner parties. President Bill Clinton loved it so much that I had it on the table every time we celebrated his birthday. But of course for him I had to substitute nondairy whipped topping for the whipped cream.

The main ingredient is puff pastry, which you can either buy or make yourself. It is so much fun to make puff pastry that I would recommend that this is the way you should go. The puff pastry has to be made at least a day in advance so that it has a chance to rest. The dough freezes very well for up to 2 months, and can be used for many other things. Make a full recipe and you will be able to produce beautiful hors d'oeuvres and delicate pastries in addition to this sensational cake.

HOLLANDER CAKE with SOUR CHERRIES

Serves 10

1¼ pounds homemade Puff Pastry dough (page 268) or store-bought all-butter puff pastry dough, chilled

¼ cup confectioners' sugar, plus more for dusting

2½ tablespoons cornstarch

2 tablespoons water

One 24-ounce jar sour cherries in natural juice (unsweetened)

4 tablespoons granulated sugar

½ teaspoon pure almond extract

2½ cups heavy cream

1 tablespoon pure vanilla extract

6 tablespoons strained red currant jelly

1 cup sliced almonds, toasted until golden and slightly crushed (optional)

1 recipe Lemon Glaze (page 261)

After you drain the cherries, check them for pits, which are occasionally left behind. Don't forget the red currant jelly—it adds a needed hint of acidity to the cake. Be sure to put this cake together 4 to 6 hours before serving, to allow the puff pastry to soften up a little bit (in dry climates you can assemble it up to 1 day in advance).

1. Cut the puff pastry dough into three equal pieces. Use your hands to press each piece into a 6-inch round. Refrigerate, covered, for 30 minutes.

2. Line three baking sheets with parchment paper and set them aside. Remove one piece of dough from the refrigerator and turn it out onto a lightly floured work surface. Sprinkle it with a little flour. With a lightly floured rolling pin, roll the pastry out to form an 11-inch round, rotating the dough 90 degrees with each pass of the rolling pin. Place the dough on one of the prepared baking sheets, cover with plastic wrap, and refrigerate for 1 hour. Repeat with the remaining two pieces of dough.

3. Preheat the oven to 425 degrees.

4. Remove the dough from the refrigerator, and using a 9-inch cardboard cake round or plate as a guide, trim each piece into an even round (Reserve the leftover pieces for another use, placing them in a zipper-lock bag and then freezing.) Prick each round ten or fifteen times with a fork.

5. Place in the oven and bake for 15 minutes. Lower the heat to 390 degrees. Prop the oven door open with a little ball of aluminum foil or the handle of a wooden spoon to allow steam to escape, and continue baking until the dough is very crisp and browned, another 10 to 15 minutes. Then transfer the baking sheet to a wire rack. Repeat with the remaining rounds.

6. After all three pieces are baked, turn the broiler to high. Slide one piece of puff pastry off of the parchment and back onto the baking sheet. Dust heavily with confectioners' sugar. Broil them, one at a time, until the sugar melts and caramelizes. This will take only a few seconds, so watch carefully and pull the baking sheet from the oven before the sugar begins to burn. Repeat with remaining two pieces. Allow the puff pastry to cool completely on the baking sheets.

7. Combine the cornstarch and water in a small bowl, and stir until smooth.

8. Drain the cherries in a colander set over a bowl. Transfer the juice (you should have about 1½ cups) to a small saucepan and add the granulated sugar. Bring to a boil over medium-high heat, and whisk in the cornstarch mixture. Cook, whisking constantly, until thickened, about 30 seconds. Remove the pan from the heat and stir in the almond extract and the cherries. Pour into a bowl and let cool completely.

(cont. on next page)

9. Pour the heavy cream into the bowl of an electric mixer fitted with the whisk attachment, and whip on high speed until soft peaks appear. Add the ¼ cup confectioners' sugar and the vanilla, and continue to whip until the cream just holds stiff peaks. Do not overwhip.

10. Place one of the puff pastry rounds on a cutting board, and use an 8-inch cardboard cake round or cake pan as a guide to trim it into a neat round. Repeat with the remaining puff pastry pieces. Place one of the rounds on a serving platter and spread 2 tablespoons of the red currant jelly over it.

11. Scrape the whipped cream into a pastry bag fitted with a #8 or #9 plain tip. Pipe a circle around the edge of the jelly-covered round. Pipe another circle about 1 inch inside the first circle, and then a third one inside that. Use a spoon to place cooled cherries in the spaces between the whipped cream circles.

12. Spread the second round of puff pastry with 2 tablespoons of the red currant jelly, and place it on top of the first round, pressing down lightly. Repeat the three circles of whipped cream as described above, and spoon cherries in the spaces between the whipped cream circles. Place the third puff pastry round on top, caramelized side up. Press down slightly to compact the cake.

13. Using an offset spatula, smooth the remaining whipped cream over the sides of the cake. Press the almonds into the sides of the cake, if desired.

14. Spread the remaining 2 tablespoons red currant jelly over the top layer of puff pastry. Spoon the Lemon Glaze over the jelly. Refrigerate for at least 4 hours and up to 12 hours. Let sit at room temperature for 30 to 40 minutes before serving.

INDIVIDUAL HOLLANDER CAKES

Serves 8

10 ounces homemade Puff Pastry dough (page 268) or store-bought all-butter puff pastry dough, chilled

2 tablespoons confectioners' sugar, plus more for dusting

1 tablespoon plus 1 teaspoon cornstarch

1 tablespoon water

One 12-ounce jar sour cherries in natural juice (unsweetened)

2 tablespoons granulated sugar

1/4 teaspoon pure almond extract

1 1/4 cups heavy cream

1 1/2 teaspoons pure vanilla extract

5 tablespoons plus 1 teaspoon red currant jelly

1/2 recipe Lemon Glaze (page 261)

1 recipe Vanilla Sauce (page 251)

I like to make individual versions of cakes for times when slicing a large cake would be inconvenient. The Hollander Cake adapts easily: Simply halve the ingredients and proceed as directed. Just don't prick the puff pastry rounds with a fork. With large rounds, you do this to control the puffing, so the layers stay relatively even. With the small cakes, you want a nice rounded top. I like to pipe a whipped cream rosette on top of each cake and pour a little Vanilla Sauce around each one to dress them up.

1. Line a baking sheet with parchment paper and set it aside. Turn the puff pastry out onto a lightly floured work surface. Sprinkle it with a little flour. With a lightly floured rolling pin, roll the pastry out into a rectangle about 3/16 inch thick, rotating the dough 90 degrees with each pass of the rolling pin. Place the dough on the baking sheet, cover it with plastic wrap, and refrigerate for 1 hour.

2. Preheat the oven to 425 degrees.

3. Remove the dough from the refrigerator and use a 3 1/2-inch biscuit cutter to cut out 16 rounds. Return them to the parchment-lined baking sheet. (Reserve any leftover pieces for another use, placing them in a zipper-lock bag and then freezing.) Do not prick the rounds with a fork.

4. Place the baking sheet in the oven and bake for 10 minutes. Lower the heat to 375 degrees. Prop the oven door open with a little ball of aluminum foil or the handle of a wooden spoon to allow steam to escape, and continue baking until the rounds are very crisp and browned, another 10 to 15 minutes. Transfer the baking sheet to a wire rack.

5. Turn the broiler to high. Slide one piece of puff pastry off of the parchment and back onto the baking sheet. Dust the pastry rounds heavily with confectioners' sugar. Broil until the sugar melts and caramelizes. This will take only a few seconds, so watch carefully and pull the baking sheet from the oven before the sugar begins to burn. Repeat with remaining pastry. Allow the puff pastry rounds to cool completely on the baking sheet.

6. Combine the cornstarch and water in a small bowl and stir until smooth.

7. Drain the cherries in a colander set over a bowl. Transfer the juice (you should have about ¾ cup) to a small saucepan and add the granulated sugar. Bring to a boil over medium-high heat and whisk in the cornstarch mixture. Cook, whisking constantly, until thickened, about 30 seconds. Remove the pan from the heat and stir in the almond extract and the cherries. Pour into a bowl and let cool completely.

8. Pour the heavy cream into the bowl of an electric mixer fitted with the whisk attachment, and whip on high speed until soft peaks appear. Add the 2 tablespoons confectioners' sugar and the vanilla, and continue to whip until the cream just holds stiff peaks. Do not overwhip.

(cont. on next page)

9. Select 8 of the nicest-looking pastry rounds (these will be the top layers of the cakes) and spread 1 teaspoon of the red currant jelly evenly over the top of each one. Set aside.

10. Spread 1 teaspoon of the jelly over each of the remaining 8 rounds. Scrape the whipped cream into a pastry bag fitted with a #6 plain tip, and pipe a circle of whipped cream around the edge of these 8 bottom rounds. Fill in the center of each one with some cherries. Place the remaining rounds on top, and spoon some Lemon Glaze on top of each cake. Pipe a whipped cream rosette on top of the glaze.

11. Serve immediately, or refrigerate (uncovered) for up to 5 hours before serving. To serve, transfer the cakes to individual dessert dishes, and spoon some Vanilla Sauce on the side of each cake.

BLOSSOMING HOLLANDER CAKE with HONEY VANILLA ICE CREAM

Serves 10

1¼ pounds homemade Puff Pastry dough (page 268) or store-bought all-butter puff pastry dough, chilled

1 large egg, lightly beaten

¼ cup confectioners' sugar, plus more for dusting

2½ tablespoons cornstarch

2 tablespoons water

One 24-ounce jar sour cherries in natural juice (unsweetened)

4 tablespoons granulated sugar

½ teaspoon almond extract

2½ cups heavy cream

1 tablespoon pure vanilla extract

4 tablespoons strained red currant jelly

½ cup sliced almonds, toasted until golden and slightly crushed (optional)

1 recipe Honey Vanilla Ice Cream (page 253)

Decorative cuts in the top layer of the pastry in this version of the Hollander Cake make an impressive visual statement. Here, I cut large flower petals into the puff pastry so that when it bakes, the cuts open up to create a three-dimensional blossom. The Honey Vanilla Ice Cream adds a beautiful floral note, especially if made with lavender or orange blossom honey.

1. Cut the puff pastry into three equal pieces. Use your hands to press each piece into a 6-inch round. Cover with plastic wrap and refrigerate for 30 minutes.

2. Line three baking sheets with parchment paper and set them aside. Remove one piece of dough from the refrigerator and turn it out onto a lightly floured work surface. Sprinkle it with a little flour. With a lightly floured rolling pin, roll the pastry out to form an 11-inch round, rotating the dough 90 degrees with each pass of the rolling pin. Place the dough on one of the prepared baking sheets, cover with plastic wrap, and refrigerate for 1 hour. Repeat with the remaining two pieces of dough.

3. Remove the dough from the refrigerator and using a 10-inch cardboard cake round or plate as a guide, trim each piece into an even round. (Reserve the leftover pieces for another use, placing them in a zipper-lock bag and then freezing.) Prick just two of the rounds ten or fifteen times with a fork. Cover and refrigerate. Brush the third piece lightly with the beaten egg. Refrigerate, uncovered, for 45 minutes.

(cont. on next page)

4. Preheat the oven to 425 degrees.

5. With a small, sharp paring knife, draw a flower design in the egg-glazed round, cutting into the dough at a slight angle: Starting in the center, cut 8 or so evenly shaped petals, each about 7 inches long. Make a cut down the length of each petal, and then smaller diagonal cuts on either side of the lengthwise cut. Surrounding the central petals, cut more petal shapes so that they look as if they are underneath the central petals and the whole design resembles a flower that is opening up. When baked, the cuts in the dough will open up to reveal the flower.

6. Place the baking sheet in the oven and bake for 15 minutes. Lower the heat to 390 degrees. Prop the oven door open with a little ball of aluminum foil or the handle of a wooden spoon to allow steam to escape, and continue baking until the dough is very crisp and browned, another 10 to 15 minutes. Transfer the baking sheet to a wire rack. Repeat with the two plain rounds.

7. After all three pieces are baked, turn the broiler to high. Slide one piece of puff pastry off of the parchment and back onto the baking sheet. Dust each piece of pastry heavily with confectioners' sugar. Broil them, one at a time, until the sugar melts and caramelizes. This will take only a few seconds, so watch carefully and pull the baking sheet from the oven before the sugar begins to burn. Repeat with remaining pastry. Allow the puff pastry to cool completely on the baking sheets.

8. Combine the cornstarch and water in a small bowl and stir until smooth.

9. Drain the cherries in a colander set over a bowl. Transfer the juice (you should have about 1½ cups) to a small saucepan and add the granulated sugar. Bring to a boil over medium-high heat, and whisk in the cornstarch mixture. Cook, whisking constantly, until thickened, about 30 seconds. Remove the pan from the heat, and stir in the almond extract and the cherries. Pour into a bowl and let cool completely.

10. Pour the heavy cream into the bowl of an electric mixer fitted with the whisk attachment, and whip on high speed until soft peaks appear. Add the ¼ cup confectioners' sugar and the vanilla, and continue to whip until the cream just holds stiff peaks. Do not overwhip.

11. Set aside the puff pastry piece with the decorative cuts; it will be the top of the cake. Place one of the other rounds on a serving platter and spread 2 tablespoons of the red currant jelly over it.

12. Scrape the whipped cream into a pastry bag fitted with a #8 or #9 plain tip. Pipe a circle around the edge of the jelly-covered round. Pipe another circle about 1 inch inside the first circle, and then a third one inside that. Use a spoon to place cooled cherries in the spaces between the whipped cream circles.

(cont. on next page)

13. Spread the second plain round of puff pastry with the remaining 2 tablespoons red currant jelly, and place it on top, pressing down lightly. Repeat piping the whipped cream and placing the cherries as before. Place the "blossoming" puff pastry round on top, and press down slightly to compact the cake.

14. Smooth the remaining whipped cream over the sides of the cake, using an offset spatula. Press the almonds into the sides of the cake if desired. Refrigerate (uncovered) for at least 4 hours and up to 12 hours. Let sit at room temperature for 30 minutes before serving with Honey Vanilla Ice Cream on the side.

20. AURORA PACIFICA

Here is a cake—a beautiful scallop-shaped puff pastry shell
filled with ginger mousse—that I used frequently at the
White House whenever a marine theme was appropriate. I
served it to the prime minister of Australia and to Jacques
Cousteau, among many others. Just recently, I made it for a
group of food writers at the annual International Association
of Cooking Professionals in Seattle, in honor of the sunset
over the Pacific.

The puff pastry here is rolled much thicker than in the
Hollander Cake because it is sliced and filled, rather than
used as cake layers. As with the individual Hollander Cakes,
don't prick it with a fork before baking, so you get a very
puffy shell.

AURORA PACIFICA with FRESH BERRIES

Serves 10

FOR THE PUFF PASTRY
SHELL:

1¼ pounds homemade Puff
Pastry dough (page 268) or
store-bought all-butter puff
pastry dough, chilled

1 egg, lightly beaten

Confectioners' sugar for
dusting

FOR THE GINGER MOUSSE:

5½ tablespoons granulated
sugar

3 tablespoons cornstarch

3 large egg yolks

1½ cups whole milk

2 teaspoons ground ginger

1½ teaspoons pure vanilla
extract

Pinch salt

3 tablespoons unsalted butter

1 cup heavy cream

2 tablespoons water

1 teaspoon unflavored gelatin

⅓ cup crystallized ginger, cut
into very thin slivers

**The ginger in the mousse gives this dessert an Asian flavor.
I use ground ginger because I can control the intensity of
the flavor with it, adding more if I need to. Sometimes fresh
ginger can be harsh-tasting and overly strong. A sprinkling of
crystallized ginger in the whipped cream adds crunch and a
little spice.**

1. Make the puff pastry shell: Line a baking sheet with
parchment paper and set it aside. Use your hands to press
the puff pastry dough into a rough 8-inch round. Wrap it in
plastic wrap and refrigerate for 1 hour.

2. Remove the dough from the refrigerator and turn it
out onto a lightly floured work surface. Sprinkle it with
a little flour. With a lightly floured rolling pin, roll the
pastry out to form an 11-inch round, rotating the dough
90 degrees each pass of the rolling pin. Place the dough
on the prepared baking sheet, cover with plastic wrap, and
refrigerate for 1 hour.

3. Remove the dough from the refrigerator, and using a
10-inch cardboard cake round or plate as a guide, trim the
dough to form an even round. You should have no more
than a couple of ounces of dough left over. You want your
dough round to be nice and thick. (Reserve leftover pieces
for another use, placing them in a zipper-lock bag and then
freezing.)

3 tablespoons orange
marmalade or jam of your
choice

1 pint blueberries, washed
and patted dry

$1/2$ pint raspberries

8 large strawberries, washed,
allowed to air-dry, stemmed,
and sliced

4. Brush the puff pastry lightly with the beaten egg.
Refrigerate, uncovered, for 45 minutes.

5. Preheat the oven to 425 degrees.

6. With a small, sharp paring knife, cutting into the dough
at a slight angle, draw your design: Draw lines radiating from
one point on the edge of the round to the edges, fanning
outward, to look like the fanned ridges on a scallop shell.
Then cut scallop lines to connect the fan lines, to look like
the ridges along the edge of the shell. When baked, the cuts
in the dough will open up to reveal the design.

7. Place the baking sheet in the oven and bake for 15
minutes. Lower the heat to 390 degrees. Prop the oven door
open with a little ball of aluminum foil or the handle of a
wooden spoon to allow steam to escape, and continue baking
until the dough is very crisp and browned, 15 to 20 minutes
more. Then transfer the baking sheet to a wire rack.

8. Turn the broiler to high. Slide puff pastry off of the
parchment and back onto the baking sheet. Dust the top of
the puff pastry heavily with confectioners' sugar, and broil
until the sugar melts and caramelizes. This will take only a
few seconds, so watch carefully, moving the baking sheet if
one spot is browning more quickly than the rest and pulling
the baking sheet from the oven before the sugar begins to
burn. The glaze should be dark mahogany, but not black.
Allow the puff pastry to cool completely on the baking
sheet, about 30 minutes. (You can let the pastry stand at

(cont. on next page)

room temperature for up to 1 day, but if you aren't going to use it within a few hours, slice the shell in half horizontally with a sharp serrated knife. If you wait until the next day to do this, the center of the shell will have become brittle and the shell may shatter.)

9. Make the ginger mousse: Whisk the sugar and cornstarch together in a medium bowl. Whisk in the egg yolks.

10. Combine the milk and ground ginger in a large saucepan, and bring to a boil. Slowly dribble ½ cup of the hot milk mixture into the egg mixture, whisking constantly. Dribble another ½ cup of the milk into the egg mixture, again whisking constantly.

11. Whisk the egg mixture back into the milk and return the pan to the heat. Bring to a full boil, whisking constantly. Remove the pan from the heat and pour the mixture through a fine-mesh sieve into a bowl. Stir in the vanilla, salt, and butter. Allow to cool completely. Then cover with plastic wrap and refrigerate for up to 2 days.

12. Pour the heavy cream into the bowl of an electric mixer fitted with the whisk attachment, and whip until it just holds stiff peaks. Set aside.

13. Pour 1 inch of water into a small saucepan and bring to a bare simmer. Pour the 2 tablespoons water into a small heatproof bowl, sprinkle the gelatin on top, and let stand to dissolve. Then place the bowl over the simmering water and heat, whisking constantly, just until the gelatin softens and melts, 30 seconds to 1 minute.

14. Whisk the melted gelatin into the ginger cream, working quickly so that no rubbery strands form. Add the whipped cream and the crystallized ginger, and fold together, taking care not to deflate the whipped cream.

15. Assemble the cake: Use a sharp serrated knife to cut the puff pastry shell in half horizontally. Spread the marmalade in an even layer over the bottom half of the shell. Place the bottom half in the center of a large serving platter.

16. Smooth half of the ginger mousse over the marmalade. Arrange half of the blueberries and half of the raspberries on top of the mousse. Reserving 1 cup of the mousse, smooth the remaining mousse over the berries. Arrange the remaining blueberries and raspberries on top. Set the top of the puff pastry shell in place, pressing down on one side so that it looks as if the shell is opening up. Smooth the reserved ginger mousse over any exposed berries in the opening.

17. Press the sliced strawberries, points facing up, in the exposed mousse between the top and bottom shells. Serve immediately, or let stand at room temperature for up to 1 hour before serving. Or refrigerate (uncovered) for up to 1 day before serving.

AURORA PACIFICA with LEMON CREAM "SEAFOAM"

Serves 10

1 Aurora Pacifica with Fresh Berries (page 210)

1 recipe Lemon Cream (page 250)

Blue food coloring

In this simple variation, Lemon Cream is colored the pale green of seafoam, and then spread in front of the cake so that it looks like a shell at the water's edge.

1. Position the cake off-center on a large rimmed platter, so there is plenty of room in front of it to spread the "ocean" of Lemon Cream.

2. Divide the Lemon Cream equally between two bowls. Add a drop or two of blue food coloring to one of the bowls, and stir to color the cream a pale sea-green.

3. Spread a line of the uncolored Lemon Cream on the platter in front of the shell. Next to this line, spread a line of green cream. Continue, alternating yellow and green until the surface of the platter in front of the shell is covered. Then drag a toothpick or skewer back and forth through the layers of cream to swirl them together, taking care not to overmix. You want the yellow and green colors to be swirled but still separate.

4. Serve immediately, or refrigerate (uncovered) for up to 1 day before serving.

AURORA PACIFICA, JACQUES COUSTEAU-STYLE

Serves 10

FOR THE PUFF PASTRY FISH:

4 or 5 ounces scraps of puff pastry dough, left over from making the Aurora Pacifica, chilled

6 to 8 whole peppercorns, cut in half

1 egg, lightly beaten

FOR THE SPUN SUGAR SEAWEED:

2 cups sugar

$^1/_2$ cup water

2 tablespoons light corn syrup

$^1/_4$ teaspoon fresh lemon juice

Blue food coloring

1 Aurora Pacifica with Lemon Cream "Seafoam" (page 214), seafoam creams reserved in their bowls

When I served this cake to Jacques Cousteau and President Reagan, I took its decoration to the logical conclusion, making an impressive screen of seaweed out of spun sugar. Little puff pastry fish, made from the leftover dough, are the final touch. You can bake the puff pastry fish along with the shell, but remove them after 10 minutes of baking—they'll cook much more quickly than the larger piece. The sugar seaweed should be made just 2 to 3 hours before serving; otherwise it will get too sticky and soft to use. Take care if you live in a humid climate or if the day is damp, because moisture in the air will make the sugar difficult to work with. It's best to make this version in an air-conditioned setting or on a nice dry day.

1. Make the puff pastry fish: Line a baking sheet with parchment paper. Roll out the puff pastry dough on a lightly floured surface to form a $^3/_{16}$-inch-thick rectangle. Place the dough on the prepared baking sheet, cover with plastic wrap, and refrigerate for 1 hour.

2. Remove the dough from the refrigerator and using a sharp paring knife or a pastry cutter, cut out 12 to 15 little fish shapes, about 2$^1/_2$ inches long and 1 inch wide. Press a peppercorn half, round side down, in the head of each fish to resemble an eye. Lightly brush the beaten egg over the fish, and refrigerate, uncovered, for 30 minutes.

(cont. on next page)

3. Preheat the oven to 400 degrees.

4. With the tip of a small, sharp paring knife, cut little V's to make scales and lines to delineate the tail on each fish. When baked, the cuts in the dough will open up to reveal the design.

5. Place the baking sheet in the oven and bake until the fish are dark golden, about 10 minutes. Remove from the oven and place the sheet on a wire rack.

6. Make the spun sugar seaweed: Using your hands, stir the sugar and water together in a pot until the mixture is homogeneous. Bring the pot over to the sink. Holding it by the handle with one hand, hold your other hand under the running water from the faucet. With your wet hand, wipe down the sides of the pot until you can't feel any sugar crystals clinging to the sides, rewetting your hand under the running water as necessary.

7. Oil a baking sheet, and fill a large bowl with ice water. Line a rimmed baking sheet with a Silpat or aluminum foil.

8. Place the pot on the stove and turn the heat to high. Partially cover the pot so that just some of the steam will be able to escape during cooking. When the mixture comes just to a boil, uncover the pot. Use a long-handled metal spoon to carefully pour the corn syrup into the center of the pot. Do not stir, and do not dribble the syrup onto the sides of the pot. Place the spoon in the center of the pot, resting the handle against the side, and leave it there until all of the corn syrup has dissolved into the sugar mixture, about 1 minute. Remove the spoon and partially cover the pot again. Allow the mixture to cook, without stirring, until it just begins to take on a little bit of yellow color and registers 308 to 310 degrees on a candy thermometer, 10 to 12 minutes.

9. Remove the pot from the heat. Pour in the lemon juice and shake the pot back and forth until the juice is incorporated. Return the pot to the stove and bring it back to a boil. Continue to cook until the mixture is a very pale yellow and registers 315 degrees on a candy thermometer, about 2 minutes. Remove the pot from the heat and dip the bottom in the ice water to stop the cooking process; let the sugar stand in the pot, still in the ice water, for 1 minute to thicken.

10. Stir a few drops of blue food coloring into the sugar until it is a deep blue-green. Use a spoon to drizzle an uneven oval, measuring 2 x 3 inches, onto the Silpat. This will be the base for your seaweed. Drizzle 6 or 7 wavy lengths of sugar on the Silpat to look like floaty pieces of seaweed; they should be different lengths, ranging from 4 to 8 inches. Let cool completely.

11. Assemble the cake: Reheat the leftover sugar by placing the pot on top of the stove and moving it quickly back and forth across the heat until it is pourable.

(cont. on next page)

12. Set the oval sugar base against the rim of a large serving platter, and place the cake on the platter so that it covers half of the sugar piece. Quickly dip the ends of the seaweed into the warm sugar and stick them onto the sugar oval so that they are upright and resemble seaweed under water. You can also glue some of the smaller pieces right to the larger pieces, so that they look like branches.

13. Use a spoon to dab a little sugar onto the back of each fish, and glue the fish to the seaweed so it looks as though they are swimming through it.

14. Decorate the platter with the Lemon Cream as described on page 214. Serve immediately, or let stand at room temperature for up to 2 hours.

Pâte à Choux

Pâte à choux, or choux paste, is a simple mixture of flour, butter, milk, and eggs that is transformed in the oven into hollow, light-as-air puffs of pastry that can be filled with pastry cream, whipped cream, ice cream, or mousse. Arranged together, filled choux puffs become beautiful cakes. Making pâte à choux is not difficult, and your technique will improve the more you practice. When preparing the pâte à choux, it is important to stir the flour in all at once and very quickly so it dissolves. This is the best way to avoid lumps, which are difficult to break up once they form.

Pipe the dough onto parchment-lined baking sheets and make sure to bake the puffs until they are golden brown and very dry on the outside. Underbaked puffs may collapse as they cool, and even if they don't, they will be unpleasantly soggy inside instead of just moist. To make sure that your puffs dry out sufficiently, prop open the oven door with the handle of a wooden spoon during the last minutes of baking, to release the moisture from the oven. Test them for doneness by pressing on one with a fingertip. It should be firm and unyielding. If it gives at all, continue to bake for a few more minutes.

21. PARIS BREST

In the 1890s, there was a Parisian pastry chef who had a shop on the route of the Tour de France between Paris and Brest. The chef created this cake, cream puffs filled with praline-flavored whipped cream and topped with sliced almonds, all in the shape of a bicycle wheel, to commemorate the race. It was an immediate success and has since become a standard of the French pastry repertoire. I've been making this one since I was a 14-year-old apprentice in Besançon. I made it many times over the years at the White House, and its eternal popularity is proof of my belief that good desserts, well made, never go out of fashion. In fact, on a recent trip to Paris I noticed that the Paris Brest is making a comeback in fashionable pastry shops. It seems that younger pastry chefs there have rediscovered the simplest choux puff cakes, ones filled with whipped cream or pastry cream.

CLASSIC PARIS BREST

Serves 12

1½ cups milk

12 tablespoons (1½ sticks) unsalted butter

½ teaspoon salt

1½ cups plus 1 tablespoon all-purpose flour

8 large eggs

1 cup sliced blanched almonds

2½ cups Pastry Cream (page 249)

½ cup hazelnut praline paste

1 cup heavy cream

Confectioners' sugar for dusting

As with all desserts made with choux paste, it is important to bake the cream puffs and the cake ring until they are very dry. If they are too moist, they might collapse. Some recipes call for scraping out the moist insides of the puffs before filling, but I love the contrast between the crisp outsides and the moist insides, and think removing this part of the puff would be to miss out on that contrast, which is what pâte à choux is all about. Hazelnut praline paste, which is a smooth, sweetened puree of hazelnuts, is available from mail-order baking supply shops (see Resources, page 283).

1. Combine the milk, butter, and salt in a large saucepan and bring to a boil over medium-high heat.

2. Remove the pan from the heat and using a wooden spatula, stir in the flour quickly and all at once. When the flour is dissolved and the mixture is smooth, return the pan to the heat and cook, stirring constantly, for 1 minute. The mixture will be quite thick, the consistency of dry mashed potatoes.

3. Transfer the mixture to the bowl of an electric mixer fitted with the paddle attachment. With the mixer on low speed, add 7 of the eggs, one at a time, mixing until each egg is just incorporated and scraping down the sides of the bowl once or twice as necessary. Do not overmix the dough, or it will become oily and will not puff in the oven the way it should. (Alternatively, you can mix the eggs in by hand with the wooden spatula.) The dough will be a thick liquid. To test for the proper consistency, spoon some up on your wooden spatula and tip the spatula to see how fast it runs down the flat surface. It should run very slowly. If it is too thick and not running at all, stir in a little water, a tablespoon at a time, until it is a little bit looser.

4. Cover the bowl with a damp kitchen towel and let the choux paste stand at room temperature until ready to use, up to 6 hours.

5. Preheat the oven to 400 degrees. Using a dark pencil, draw an 8-inch circle on one half of a piece of parchment paper, leaving the other half blank. Turn the parchment over onto a baking sheet, so the pencil side is down. Lightly beat the remaining egg in a small bowl.

6. Fit a large pastry bag with a plain #7 tip, and fill it with the choux paste. Pipe a circle of choux paste on the parchment along the outside of the drawn circle. Pipe another circle of choux paste around the outside of the first circle. Pipe a third circle on top, along the line between the first two circles, creating a pyramidal ring.

7. On the empty half of the parchment, pipe 18 walnut-size spheres.

8. Use a pastry brush to brush a very thin coating of beaten egg all over the ring and the spheres. Moisten the tines of a fork with water, and lightly drag the tines through the egg wash on the ring to make a design. Sprinkle the almonds over the ring, lightly pressing them into the egg wash. Place the baking sheet in the oven and bake until the small puffs have doubled in size and are crisp and light golden, 15 to 20 minutes. Use a spatula to transfer the puffs to a wire rack to cool.

(cont. on next page)

9. Prop the oven door open with a little ball of aluminum foil or the handle of a wooden spoon, and continue baking the ring until it is light golden and puffed, another 15 to 20 minutes. If the almonds are browning too quickly, cover the ring with a piece of parchment paper. Transfer the ring to a wire rack, and let it cool completely.

10. Whisk the Pastry Cream and the praline paste together in a large bowl. Pour the heavy cream into the bowl of an electric mixer fitted with the whisk attachment, and whip until it holds stiff peaks. Gently fold it into the pastry cream mixture.

11. Slice the cooled pastry ring in half horizontally, using a sharp serrated knife. Place the bottom half on a serving platter. Do not scrape away the inside of the pastry. Fit a large pastry bag with a #6 or #7 star tip, and fill it with the pastry cream mixture. Pipe half of the mixture over the bottom of the pastry ring, using a back-and-forth motion so that the whole surface is covered and the pastry cream mixture extends just over the edge of the pastry, by no more than ¼ inch.

12. Slice the cooled pastry puffs in half horizontally. Place them on top of the cream-covered ring, overlapping them slightly like dominoes. Pipe more cream mixture on top of the puffs to cover. Place the top of the pastry ring on top of the covered cream puff halves. Serve immediately, or refrigerate for up to 1 day. Dust with confectioners' sugar just before serving.

LANCE ARMSTRONG'S PARIS BREST

Serves 12

1 recipe Classic Paris Brest (page 222, Steps 1–7)

2 cups French peanuts (see headnote), lightly crushed

¹/₂ cup Concord grape jelly

1 recipe Peanut Butter Cream (page 254)

Confectioners' sugar for dusting

6 or 7 Chocolate Bicyclists (page 282)

1 recipe Vanilla Sauce (page 251)

When the American cycling champion Lance Armstrong visited the White House, I came up with this Americanized version of the Paris Brest in his honor. In place of the sliced almonds, I use the delicious French peanuts (sometimes called burnt peanuts), the ones with the red candy coating. Look for them at the candy store or in the candy aisle of the supermarket. (They can also be mail-ordered; see Resources, page 283.) To crush the peanuts, put them in a zipper-lock bag and roll a rolling pin over the bag. Crush them just enough so that they break into pieces. You don't want them pulverized or turned to dust. If you like a lot of crunch, leave 1 cup of the nuts whole and use those on top of the choux paste ring.

1. Use a pastry brush to brush a very thin coating of beaten egg all over the ring and the spheres. Moisten the tines of a fork with water, and lightly drag the tines through the egg wash on the ring to create a design. Sprinkle 1 cup of the peanuts over the ring. Place the baking sheet in the oven and bake until the small puffs are doubled in size and are light golden, 15 to 20 minutes. Use a spatula to transfer the puffs to a wire rack to cool. Prop the oven door open with a small ball of aluminum foil or the handle of a wooden spoon, and continue baking the ring until it is puffed and golden, another 15 to 20 minutes. If the peanuts are browning too quickly, cover the cake with a piece of parchment paper. Transfer the ring to a wire rack and let it cool completely.

(cont. on next page)

2. Slice the cooled pastry ring in half horizontally, using a sharp serrated knife. Place the bottom half on a serving platter. Do not scrape away the inside of the cake.

3. Spread ¼ cup of the jelly over the bottom half. Fit a large pastry bag with a #6 or #7 star tip, and fill it with the Peanut Butter Cream. Pipe half of the cream over the bottom of the pastry ring, using a back-and-forth motion so that the whole surface is covered and the cream mixture extends just over the edge of the pastry, by no more than ¼ inch. Sprinkle with ½ cup of the French peanuts.

4. Slice the cooled pastry puffs in half horizontally. Spread a little of the remaining jelly on the bottom of each half. Place them on top of the cream-covered ring, overlapping them slightly like dominoes. Pipe more cream on top of the puffs to cover. Sprinkle with the remaining ½ cup of French peanuts. Place the top of the pastry ring on top of the cream puffs. Just before serving, dust with confectioners' sugar and arrange the Chocolate Bicyclists around the Paris Brest. Serve with the Vanilla Sauce on the side.

PARIS BREST with CHESTNUTS and CHOCOLATE SAUCE

Serves 12

1 recipe Classic Paris Brest
(page 222, Steps 1–10)

1½ cups chestnuts in syrup,
drained and coarsely chopped

Confectioners' sugar for
dusting

1 recipe Light Chocolate
Sauce (page 260), at room
temperature

When President George W. Bush came to the White House in 2001, I quickly discovered his preference for all-American layer cakes, but I wondered what would happen if I served him this very French dessert. Knowing how he loves chocolate, I thought I could make a version that he would enjoy, so I gave it a try for a family dinner. When the cake was served by the White House butler, the President looked at it skeptically and took a small portion, helping himself to a generous serving of the sauce. The butler proceeded to serve the First Lady and then everyone else and began to leave the dining room. But before he had reached the door, the President called him back and said, "Why don't you give me another piece so you don't have to come back?" When the butler reported what had happened, I knew I had a winner. When I make this for my own family and friends, I serve it with small glasses of Amaretto or another almond liqueur.

Canned chestnuts in syrup (do not use water-packed chestnuts or fresh chestnuts) can be found in gourmet and specialty foods shops and are available by mail order (see Resources, page 283).

1. Slice the cooled pastry ring in half horizontally, using a sharp serrated knife. Place the bottom half on a serving platter. Do not scrape away the inside of the cake. Fit a large pastry bag with a #6 or #7 star tip, and fill it with the pastry cream mixture. Pipe half of the mixture over the bottom of the pastry ring, using a back-and-forth motion so that the whole surface is covered and the pastry cream mixture extends just over the edge of the pastry, by no more than ¼ inch. Sprinkle the chopped chestnuts over the pastry cream mixture.

2. Slice the cooled pastry puffs in half horizontally. Place the puffs on top of the cream-covered ring, overlapping them slightly like dominoes. Cover with the cream mixture. Place the top of the pastry ring on top of the cream puffs. Serve immediately, or refrigerate for up to 1 day before serving.

3. Just before serving, dust with confectioners' sugar. Place the Light Chocolate Sauce in a bowl that will fit in the center of the cake.

22. CROQUEMBOUCHE

The croquembouche is a classic French cake, made with custard-filled cream puffs that are dipped in caramel and stacked on top of one another. In its simpler forms, decorated with glazed fruit or Jordan almonds, it is a typical pastry shop item. Bedecked with sugar roses, ribbons, and blown sugar lovebirds, it is served at christenings, baptisms, and especially at weddings. Traditional croquembouches are built either freehand or around a special mold manufactured for the purpose. It can be nerve-wracking to build one without a mold, and disappointing when your hard work results in a lopsided cake. However, I tossed away my croquembouche molds long ago, when I came up with the idea of building my cake around either a specially baked cookie base or a block of frozen mousse or Bavarian. I love how the cookies and mousse add flavor and texture to the finished cake as well as provide stability.

MINI-CROQUEMBOUCHES

Serves 8

FOR THE RASPBERRY MOUSSE:

Two 12-ounce bags frozen sweetened raspberries, thawed

3 tablespoons cold water

$1\frac{1}{2}$ envelopes unflavored gelatin

$1\frac{1}{2}$ cups heavy cream, chilled

FOR THE CREAM PUFFS:

1 cup milk

8 tablespoons unsalted butter

$\frac{1}{2}$ teaspoon salt

1 cup plus $\frac{1}{2}$ tablespoon all-purpose flour

4 large eggs

1 large egg yolk

1 large egg, lightly beaten

$2\frac{1}{2}$ cups Pastry Cream (page 249), chilled

3 tablespoons fruit-flavored liqueur, such as Chambord or Grand Marnier (optional)

This is the simplest way to make this cake: using demitasse cups to mold individual portions of mousse and then arranging tiny cream puffs around each one, to produce 8 mini-croquembouches. I use raspberry mousse in this recipe, but any favorite frozen mousse or Bavarian will serve the purpose. (In *Dessert University,* you'll find many Bavarian variations that I use for this cake.) Once put together, the cakes can be served immediately, with the mousse inside still slightly frozen (it will begin to defrost as you work), or they can sit on the counter for up to 2 hours before serving, in which case the mousse will thaw completely and be soft.

1. Make the raspberry mousse: Place the defrosted raspberries in a blender or in a food processor, and puree until smooth. Push the puree through a fine-mesh strainer into a bowl to remove the seeds. Measure out 2 cups of the puree and place it in a bowl; reserve any remaining puree for another use.

2. Pour 1 inch of water into a small saucepan and bring to a bare simmer. Pour the cold water into a small bowl and sprinkle the gelatin on top. Let stand to dissolve. Then place the bowl on top of the simmering water and heat, whisking constantly, just until the gelatin melts, 30 seconds to 1 minute. Whisk the softened gelatin into the puree, working quickly so that no rubbery strands form.

FOR THE CARAMEL GLAZE:

1 cup sanding sugar (see Resources, page 283)

2 cups sugar

1/2 cup water

2 tablespoons light corn syrup

1/4 teaspoon fresh lemon juice

Fresh raspberries for garnish

3. Pour the cream into the bowl of an electric mixer fitted with the whisk attachment, and whip until it holds soft peaks. Fold the raspberry puree into the whipped cream. Divide the mixture among eight demitasse cups or small teacups, measuring about 2½ inches deep and 2 inches wide. Smooth the tops with a spatula. Cover each cup with plastic wrap and freeze for at least 6 hours and up to 3 weeks.

4. Make the cream puffs: Preheat the oven to 425 degrees. Combine the milk, butter, and salt in a large saucepan and bring to a boil over medium-high heat.

5. Remove the pan from the heat and using a wooden spatula, stir in the flour quickly and all at once. When the flour is dissolved and the mixture is smooth, return the pan to the heat and cook, stirring constantly, for 1 minute. The mixture will be quite thick, the consistency of dry mashed potatoes.

6. Transfer the mixture to the bowl of an electric mixer fitted with the paddle attachment. With the mixer on low speed, add the whole eggs and then the yolk, one at a time, mixing until each egg is just incorporated and scraping down the sides of the bowl once or twice as necessary. Do not overmix the dough, or it will become oily and will not puff in the oven the way it should. (Alternatively, you can mix the eggs in by hand with the wooden spatula.) The dough will be a thick liquid. To test for the proper consistency, spoon some up on

(cont. on next page)

your wooden spatula and tip the spatula to see how fast it runs down the flat surface. It should run very slowly. If it is too thick and not running at all, stir in a little water, a tablespoon at a time, until it is a little bit looser.

7. Use the pâte à choux right away, or cover the bowl with a damp kitchen towel and let it stand at room temperature until ready to use, up to 6 hours.

8. Line two baking sheets with parchment paper. Scrape the choux paste into a pastry bag fitted with a plain #6 or #7 tip. Pipe about 64 spheres, each about the size of a walnut, spacing them about 1½ inches apart, on the parchment paper. Brush them lightly with the beaten egg, and then gently drag the tines of a fork through the egg to make a design. Place the baking sheets in the oven, and prop the oven door open with a small ball of aluminum foil or the handle of a wooden spoon (this will help prevent the puffs from collapsing). Bake until the puff are golden brown, 10 to 15 minutes. Remove from the oven and cool completely on the baking sheets.

9. Fill the cream puffs: Combine the Pastry Cream with the liqueur, if desired. Using the tip of a paring knife, make a twisting motion to create a small hole, about the diameter of a pencil, in the bottom of each puff. Fit a pastry bag with a #3 or #4 plain tip, fill it with the Pastry Cream, and pipe it into the puffs. Make sure they are nice and full. Set them aside on a baking sheet.

10. Prepare the caramel glaze: Line a baking sheet with aluminum foil or a Silpat, and spread the sanding sugar over it. Line another baking sheet with parchment paper or another Silpat. Using your hands, stir the sugar and water together in a pot until the mixture is homogeneous. Bring the pot over to the sink. Hold it by the handle with one hand and hold your other hand under the running water from the faucet. With your wet hand, wipe down the sides of the pot until you can't feel any sugar crystals clinging to the sides, rewetting your hand under the running water as necessary.

11. Fill a large bowl with ice water and set it near the stove. Place the pot on the stove and turn the heat to high. Partially cover the pot so that just some of the steam will be able to escape during cooking. When the mixture just comes to a boil, uncover the pot. Use a long-handled metal spoon to carefully pour the corn syrup into the middle of the pot. Do not stir, and do not dribble the syrup onto the sides of the pot. Place the spoon in the middle of the pot, resting the handle against the side, and leave it there until all of the corn syrup has dissolved into the sugar mixture, about 1 minute. Remove the spoon and partially cover the pot again. Allow to cook, without stirring, until the mixture just begins to take on a little bit of yellow color and registers 308 to 310 degrees on a candy thermometer, 10 to 12 minutes.

(cont. on next page)

12. Remove the pot from the heat. Pour in the lemon juice and shake the pot back and forth until the lemon juice is incorporated. Return the pot to the stove and bring back to a boil. Continue to cook until the mixture is a very pale yellow and registers 315 degrees on a candy thermometer, about 2 minutes.

13. Remove the pot from the heat and dip the bottom in the ice water to stop the cooking process. Let the sugar stand in the pot, still in the ice water, for 1 minute to thicken.

14. Put a folded kitchen towel underneath one side of the pot, so that it tilts and the sugar pools in the lower portion.

15. Dip a cream puff halfway into the cooked sugar. Shake, and scrape off the excess sugar on the edge of the pot. Dip the sugar-covered portion in the sanding sugar. Place the puff on the parchment-lined baking sheet. Repeat with the remaining puffs. If the sugar becomes too thick, rewarm it on the stove by moving the bottom of the pot quickly back and forth across the heat or by putting the pot in a 375-degree oven for 5 minutes.

16. Assemble the mini-croquemboches: Remove the raspberry mousses from the freezer and unwrap them. Unmold each mousse by dipping the cup in hot water for 5 to 10 seconds, running a paring knife around the perimeter of the cup, and then inverting the mousse onto a dessert plate. Let stand for 15 or 20 minutes so that the surface softens slightly.

17. Arrange 6 to 8 cream puffs all around and over each mousse, sugar sides facing out, to completely cover it; press the unglazed sides into the mousse slightly so they adhere. Serve immediately, while the mousse is still slightly frozen, or let stand until the mousse defrosts, up to 2 hours. Garnish each plate with a few raspberries before serving.

LARGE CROQUEMBOUCHE

Serves 25

FOR THE LANGUE DE CHAT CONE:

2 cups (4 sticks) unsalted butter, at room temperature

2 cups confectioners' sugar

1 tablespoon pure vanilla extract

2 tablespoons grated lemon zest

$1/4$ teaspoon salt

8 large egg whites, at room temperature, lightly beaten

$1^1/3$ cups all-purpose flour

FOR THE CREAM PUFFS:

2 cups milk

1 cup (2 sticks) unsalted butter

1 teaspoon salt

2 cups plus 2 tablespoons all-purpose flour

8 large eggs

2 large egg yolks

2 large eggs, lightly beaten

5 cups Pastry Cream (page 249), chilled

If you have some experience with cream puffs and are ready for a challenge, you might want to try this large croquembouche, guaranteed to impress a crowd at a large party—a christening, anniversary, wedding shower, or any other happy occasion. For this one, I make a mold out of langue de chat dough that has been baked around a foil-covered Styrofoam cone from the craft store. It's another way to make an even, beautiful cake without a croquembouche mold. On the slight chance that your cookie mold breaks, have a second one ready. There's enough batter in the recipe to make two.

1. Make the langue de chat mold: Preheat the oven to 375 degrees. Wrap a Styrofoam cone no taller than 12 inches (its total surface area shouldn't be bigger than a sheet pan) with heavy-duty aluminum foil. Wrap a piece of parchment paper around the cone to measure its surface area, and cut the paper into a triangle that measures the same as the surface area of the cone, leaving an extra inch along one long edge. Place the paper triangle on a $1/8$-inch-thick piece of cardboard, and trace around it. Cut the triangle out of the center of the cardboard. This will be the stencil for your langue de chat base.

2. Combine the butter, confectioners' sugar, vanilla, lemon zest, and salt in the bowl of an electric mixer fitted with the paddle attachment. Mix on medium speed until smooth.

¼ cup fruit-flavored liqueur, such as Chambord or Grand Marnier, optional

FOR THE CARAMEL GLAZE:

4 cups sugar

1 cup water

¼ cup light corn syrup

½ teaspoon fresh lemon juice

---

1 cup sanding sugar (see Resources, page 283)

2 cups Jordan almonds for garnish

3. With the mixer running on medium-high speed, alternately add a tablespoon of egg white and a tablespoon of flour until all of the egg whites and flour are incorporated and the batter is smooth.

4. Line two baking sheets with parchment paper. Place the stencil on one of the baking sheets. Drop 1 to 1½ cups of the batter inside the stencil, and use a small offset spatula to smooth the batter to the edges of the cutout triangle. Carefully lift the stencil straight up and away from the baking sheet so that you leave a neat triangle of batter on the parchment. Repeat with the remaining batter on the second baking sheet. (You will have enough batter to make two cookie bases, just in case!)

5. Bake until the edges of the triangles are light brown, 7 to 9 minutes. When the first sheet comes out of the oven, lay the foil-wrapped cone on its side at one side of the cookie triangle. Use a spatula and your fingers to lift the edge of the cookie onto the cone, and then roll the cone toward the other side of the triangle so that it is completely covered by the cookie. The edges of the cookie should overlap slightly. Stand the cone on a wire rack. If the bottom edge is uneven, trim it with a sharp serrated knife while the cookie is still soft. If you tear or break the cookie, try again with the back-up sheet.

6. Make the cream puffs: Preheat the oven to 425 degrees. Combine the milk, butter, and salt in a large saucepan and bring to a boil over medium-high heat.

(cont. on next page)

7. Remove the pan from the heat, and using a wooden spatula, stir in the flour quickly and all at once. When the flour is dissolved and the mixture is smooth, return the pan to the heat and cook, stirring constantly, for 1 minute. The mixture will be quite thick, the consistency of dry mashed potatoes.

8. Transfer the mixture to the bowl of an electric mixer fitted with the paddle attachment. With the mixer on low speed, add the whole eggs and then the yolks, one at a time, mixing until each egg is just incorporated and scraping down the sides of the bowl once or twice as necessary. Do not overmix the dough, or it will become oily and will not puff in the oven the way it should. (Alternatively, you can mix the eggs in by hand with the wooden spatula.) The dough will be a thick liquid. To test for the proper consistency, spoon some onto your wooden spatula and tip the spatula to see how fast it runs down the flat surface. It should run very slowly. If it is too thick and not running at all, stir in a little water, a tablespoon at a time, until it is a little bit looser.

9. Use the pâte à choux right away, or cover the bowl with a damp kitchen towel and let it stand at room temperature until ready to use, up to 6 hours.

10. Line two baking sheets with parchment paper. Scrape some of the choux paste into a pastry bag fitted with a plain #6 or #7 tip. Pipe 60 or so spheres, each about the size of a walnut, spacing them about 1½ inches apart, on the sheet. Brush lightly with the beaten eggs, and then gently drag the tines of a fork through the egg wash to create a design. Place the baking sheets in the oven, and prop the oven door open with a small ball of aluminum foil or the handle of a wooden spoon (this will help prevent the puffs from collapsing). Bake until golden brown, 10 to 15 minutes. Remove from the oven and cool completely on the baking sheet. Repeat with the remaining choux paste.

11. When they have cooled completely, fill the cream puffs: Combine the Pastry Cream with the liqueur, if desired. Using the tip of a paring knife, make a twisting motion to create a small hole, about the diameter of a pencil, in the bottom of each puff. Fit a pastry bag with a #3 or #4 plain tip, fill it with the Pastry Cream, and pipe it into the puffs. Make sure they are nice and full. Set aside on a baking sheet.

12. Prepare the caramel glaze: Line two baking sheets with parchment paper or Silpats. Using your hands, stir the sugar and water together in a pot until the mixture is homogeneous. Bring the pot over to the sink. Hold it by the handle with one hand and hold your other hand under the running water from the faucet. With your wet hand, wipe down the sides of the pot until you can't feel any sugar crystals clinging to the sides, rewetting your hand under the running water as necessary.

13. Fill a large bowl with ice water and set it near the stove. Place the pot on the stove and turn the heat to high. Partially cover the pot so that just some of the steam will be able to escape during cooking. When the mixture just comes to a boil, uncover the pot. Use a long-handled metal spoon to carefully pour the corn syrup into the middle of the sugar

(cont. on next page)

mixture. Do not stir, and do not dribble the syrup onto the sides of the pot. Place the spoon in the middle of the pot, resting the handle against the side, and leave it there until all of the corn syrup has dissolved into the sugar mixture, about 1 minute. Remove the spoon and partially cover again. Allow to cook, without stirring, until the mixture just begins to take on a little bit of yellow color and registers 308 to 310 degrees on a candy thermometer, 10 to 12 minutes.

14. Remove the pot from the heat. Pour in the lemon juice and shake the pot back and forth until the lemon juice is incorporated. Return the pot to the stove and bring back to a boil. Continue to cook until the mixture is a very pale yellow and registers 315 degrees on a candy thermometer, about 2 minutes.

15. Remove the pot from the heat and dip the bottom in the ice water to stop the cooking process. Let the cooked sugar stand in the pot, still in the ice water, for 1 minute to thicken.

16. Put a folded kitchen towel under one side of the pot, so that it tilts and the sugar pools in the lower portion.

17. Dip a cream puff halfway into the hot cooked sugar. Shake it, and scrape off the excess sugar on the edge of the pot. Dip the sugar-covered portion in the sanding sugar. Place it on the parchment-lined baking sheet. Repeat with the remaining puffs. If the cooked sugar becomes too thick, rewarm it on the stove by moving the bottom of the pot quickly back and forth across the heat or by putting the pot in a 375-degree oven for 5 minutes.

18. Assemble the croquemboche: Carefully slide the langue de chat cone off its Styrofoam base. Use a little leftover cooked sugar to anchor the cone to a serving platter. Starting at the bottom, arrange the cream puffs in concentric circles around the cone, dipping the bottom of each puff in a little cooked sugar and sticking it on the cone so the sugar-covered half of the puff is facing outward.

19. Dip the ends of the Jordan almonds into the caramel and then affix them to the croquemboche randomly, wherever there is a space. Serve immediately, or let stand at room temperature for 4 to 5 hours before serving.

WEDDING CROQUEMBOUCHE

Serves 30

FOR THE RASPBERRY MOUSSE:

Three 12-ounce bags frozen sweetened raspberries

$\frac{1}{2}$ cup cold water

3 envelopes unflavored gelatin

2 cups heavy cream, chilled

1 pint raspberries

FOR THE CREAM PUFFS:

2 cups milk

1 cup (2 sticks) unsalted butter

1 teaspoon salt

2 cups plus 1 tablespoon all-purpose four

8 large eggs

2 large egg yolks

2 large eggs, lightly beaten

5 cups Pastry Cream (page 249), chilled

$\frac{1}{4}$ cup fruit-flavored liqueur such as Chambord or Grand Marnier, optional

In France, the croquembouche is the traditional wedding cake. At large weddings, you will see ones so tall that they reach the ceiling. We love them for their elegance, lightness, and rich flavors. I wish more Americans would choose this wonderful way to celebrate their nuptials—and maybe you will, once you read this recipe and see how practical it is to make at home. In fact, it's one of the quickest and easiest small wedding cakes to produce on your own. I know this from experience: When I was a young apprentice in France, the head baker entrusted me one morning to deliver two of them, by bicycle, to a nearby home where a wedding would be taking place that afternoon. Swerving so I wouldn't collide with an elderly lady walking her dog, I lost my balance and the cakes flew out of the bike baskets. After I got a serious scolding from both the lady and my boss, I got to work replacing the cakes, and had new ones ready to deliver before the ceremony was over.

This cake, like the mini-croquembouches, has a fruit mousse base. With a column of mousse this size, it's important to stabilize it with plenty of gelatin; you don't want it collapsing before it is served. The decoration can be simple and elegant: Alternating cream puffs are covered in coarse sanding sugar and candied rose petals. (More experienced pastry chefs may attempt a more elaborate finish. See photo insert.) The cake, thus embellished, is a vision of romance.

FOR THE CARAMEL GLAZE:

1 cup sanding sugar (see Resources, page 283)

4 cups sugar

2 cups water

¼ cup light corn syrup

½ teaspoon fresh lemon juice

- -

2 cups coarse sanding sugar (see Resources, page 283)

2 cups candied rose petals (see Resources, page 283)

1. Make the raspberry mousse: Have ready three round plastic containers, one measuring 6 inches in diameter and 3 inches deep, one 5 inches in diameter and 4½ inches deep, and one 2½ inches in diameter and 1 inch deep.

2. Place the frozen raspberries in a blender or in a food processor and puree until smooth. Push the puree through a fine-mesh strainer into a bowl to remove the seeds. Measure out 4 cups of the puree, pour it into a bowl, and reserve any remaining puree for another use.

3. Pour 1 inch of water into a small saucepan and bring to a bare simmer. Pour the cold water into a small bowl and sprinkle the gelatin on top. Let stand to dissolve. Then place the bowl on top of the simmering water and heat, whisking constantly, just until the gelatin melts, 30 seconds to 1 minute. Whisk the softened gelatin into the puree, working quickly so that no rubbery strands form.

4. Pour the cream into the bowl of an electric mixer fitted with the whisk attachment, and whip until it holds soft peaks. Fold the raspberry puree into the whipped cream. Then fold in the fresh raspberries. Fill the three containers with the mousse, and smooth the tops with a spatula. Cover each container with plastic wrap and freeze for at least 6 hours and up to 3 weeks.

5. Make the cream puffs: Preheat the oven to 425 degrees. Combine the milk, butter, and salt in a large saucepan and bring to a boil over medium-high heat.

(cont. on next page)

6. Remove the pan from the heat, and using a wooden spatula, stir in the flour quickly and all at once. When the flour is dissolved and the mixture is smooth, return the pan to the heat and cook, stirring constantly, for 1 minute. The mixture will be quite thick, the consistency of dry mashed potatoes.

7. Transfer the mixture to the bowl of an electric mixer fitted with the paddle attachment. With the mixer on low speed, add the whole eggs and then the yolks, one at a time, mixing until each egg is just incorporated and scraping down the sides of the bowl once or twice as necessary. Do not overmix the dough, or it will become oily and will not puff in the oven the way it should. (Alternatively, you can mix the eggs in by hand with the wooden spatula.) The dough will be a thick liquid. To test for the proper consistency, spoon some onto your wooden spatula and tip the spatula to see how fast it runs down the flat surface. It should run very slowly. If it is too thick and not running at all, stir in a little water, a tablespoon at a time, until it is a little bit looser.

8. Use the pâte à choux right away, or cover the bowl with a damp kitchen towel and let it stand at room temperature until ready to use, up to 6 hours.

9. Line two baking sheets with parchment paper. Scrape some of the choux paste into a pastry bag fitted with a plain #6 or #7 tip. Pipe 60 spheres, each about the size of a walnut, spacing them 1½ inches apart, on one of the sheets. Brush lightly with the beaten eggs, and then gently drag the tines of a fork through the egg to create a design. Place the baking sheet in the oven and prop the oven door open with a small ball of aluminum foil or the handle of a wooden spoon (this will help prevent the puffs from collapsing). Bake until golden brown, 10 to 15 minutes. Remove from the oven and cool completely on the baking sheets. Repeat with the remaining choux paste on the second baking sheet. You should have about 120 puffs when you are done.

10. When they have cooled completely, fill the cream puffs: Combine the Pastry Cream with the liqueur, if desired. Using the tip of a paring knife, make a twisting motion to create a small hole, about the diameter of a pencil, in the bottom of each puff. Fit a pastry bag with a #3 or #4 plain tip, fill it with the Pastry Cream, and pipe it into the puffs. Make sure they are nice and full. Set aside on a baking sheet.

11. Prepare the caramel glaze: Line a baking sheet with aluminum foil or a Silpat, and spread the sanding sugar over it. Line another baking sheet with aluminum foil or another Silpat. Using your hands, stir the sugar and water together in a pot until the mixture is homogeneous. Bring the pot over to the sink. Hold it by the handle with one hand and hold your other hand under the running water from the faucet. With your wet hand, wipe down the sides of the pot until you can't feel any sugar crystals clinging to the sides, rewetting your hand under the running water as necessary.

12. Fill a large bowl with ice water and set it near the stove. Place the pot on the stove and turn the heat to high. Partially cover the pot so that just some of the steam will be

(cont. on next page)

able to escape during cooking. When the mixture just comes to a boil, uncover the pot. Use a long-handled metal spoon to carefully pour the corn syrup into the middle of the sugar mixture. Do not stir, and do not dribble the syrup onto the sides of the pot. Place the spoon in the middle of the pot, resting the handle against the side, and leave it there until all of the corn syrup has dissolved into the sugar mixture, about 1 minute. Remove the spoon and partially cover again. Allow to cook, without stirring, until the mixture just begins to take on a little bit of yellow color and registers 308 to 310 degrees on a candy thermometer, 10 to 12 minutes.

13. Remove the pot from the heat. Pour in the lemon juice and shake the pot back and forth until the lemon juice is incorporated. Return the pot to the stove and bring back to a boil. Continue to cook until the mixture is a very pale yellow and registers 315 degrees on a candy thermometer, about 2 minutes.

14. Remove the pot from the heat and dip the bottom in the ice water to stop the cooking process. Let the cooked sugar stand in the pot, still in the ice water, for 1 minute to thicken.

15. Put a folded kitchen towel under one side of the pot, so that it tilts and the sugar pools in the lower portion. Place the coarse sanding sugar and the candied rose petals in separate shallow bowls or plates.

16. Dip each puff halfway into the hot sugar. Shake, and scrape off the excess sugar on the edge of the pot. As you dip them, dip half of the sugar-covered puffs in the coarse sanding sugar and half in the candied rose petals. Place them on the prepared baking sheets, caramel sides up. If the caramel becomes too thick, rewarm it on the stove by moving the bottom of the pot quickly back and forth across the heat or by putting the pot in a 375-degree oven for 5 minutes.

17. Assemble the croquemboche: Remove the raspberry mousses from the freezer and unwrap the containers. Unmold them by dipping the containers into hot water for about 5 to 10 seconds. They should pop right out. Place the largest one in the center of a large serving platter. Place the next largest on top, and then the smallest one on the very top.

18. Starting at the bottom, arrange the cream puffs in concentric circles around the mousse, alternating sugar-coated and rose petal–coated puffs. Before you stick a puff into the mousse, dip one side in a bit of caramel, so that when you place another puff next to it, they will stick together. Serve immediately, or let stand for up to 3 hours before serving.

ETC.: FROSTINGS, FILLINGS, GLAZES, SYRUPS

SWEETENED WHIPPED CREAM

**Makes enough for
8 topping portions**

1 cup heavy cream, chilled

1½ tablespoons
confectioners' sugar

½ teaspoon pure vanilla
extract

You can use sweetened whipped cream as a garnish, of course, but it also covers and decorates cakes. If you are going to pipe it, use it right away when it is at its stiffest, or rewhip it for a few seconds to bring back its volume. Use only the largest pastry bag tips. Small tips will squeeze the air out of whipped cream.

You can add food coloring to whipped cream if you like. You can also flavor it. For chocolate whipped cream, add 2 ounces of lukewarm melted semisweet chocolate to 1 cup of room-temperature cream before whipping (icy cold cream will cause the chocolate to harden before it is incorporated). For coffee whipped cream, dissolve 2 teaspoons of instant espresso powder in 1 teaspoon hot water, and add that. For cinnamon whipped cream, just add a teaspoon of ground cinnamon.

Place the cream in the bowl of an electric mixer fitted with the whisk attachment, and whip on high speed until soft peaks appear. Add the confectioners' sugar and vanilla, and continue to whip until the cream just holds stiff peaks. Do not overwhip. Use immediately, or cover with plastic wrap and refrigerate for up to 2 hours. Hand-whip refrigerated whipped cream for a few seconds before using it.

PASTRY CREAM

Makes 5 cups

³/₄ cup plus 2 tablespoons sugar

¹/₂ cup plus 2 tablespoons cornstarch

5 large eggs, or 8 large egg yolks

1 quart whole milk

1 tablespoon pure vanilla extract

Pinch salt

4 tablespoons unsalted butter, chilled (optional)

Pastry Cream is much easier to make than Vanilla Sauce; the cornstarch offers great protection against curdling. Still, be sure to whisk quickly and to reach the whisk all the way to the bottom of the pan, or the cream will burn. Burnt Pastry Cream has a terrible taste! You can customize your Pastry Cream to taste, making it richer by using all egg yolks and adding butter. Pastry Cream will stay fresh in the refrigerator for up to 3 days. If you need only a small quantity, simply halve or quarter this recipe—it will work just fine.

1. Whisk the sugar and cornstarch together in a medium bowl. Whisk in the eggs or egg yolks.

2. Bring the milk to a boil in a large saucepan. Slowly dribble ¹/₂ cup of the hot milk into the egg mixture, whisking constantly. Dribble another ¹/₂ cup of the milk into the egg mixture, again whisking constantly.

3. Whisk the egg mixture back into the milk and return the pan to the heat. Bring to a full boil, whisking constantly. Remove the pan from the heat and pour the mixture into a bowl. Stir in the vanilla, salt, and butter if desired. Allow to cool completely. Then cover with plastic wrap and refrigerate for at least 3 hours or up to 2 days. Push the Pastry Cream through a fine-mesh strainer before using it.

LEMON CREAM

Makes about 2 cups

5 large lemons

1½ cups sugar

4 large eggs

1 cup (2 sticks) unsalted butter, cut into cubes

Lemon Cream is a big favorite of mine. I love its tart flavor and the fact that it is so versatile. It can be folded into whipped cream to make a simple mousse; it can be used to sandwich cookies together; it can fill crêpes and top fruit; and of course it makes a great cake filling. Another plus: It stays fresh in the freezer for up to 3 months.

1. Remove the zest from the lemons with a grater. Cut each lemon in half and squeeze the juice into a small bowl.

2. Combine the lemon zest, lemon juice, sugar, eggs, and butter in a heavy-bottomed medium saucepan. Bring to a boil over medium-high heat and boil for 30 seconds, whisking constantly and making sure that none of the custard is sticking to the bottom of the pan.

3. Remove from the heat and pour through a fine-mesh strainer into a nonreactive bowl. Cool to room temperature. Refrigerate Lemon Cream in an airtight container until ready to use, at least 3 hours and up to 1 week, or freeze it for up to 3 months.

VANILLA SAUCE

Makes 3 cups

¹/₂ cup sugar

5 large egg yolks

2 cups whole milk

2 vanilla beans, split
lengthwise

Vanilla Sauce adds silky richness to so many desserts. Whole vanilla beans give this version extraordinary flavor. I often pour some of the sauce around a cake as a finishing touch, to moisten the slices. Its cool creamy color also adds beauty to the presentation. I can't stress enough how important it is to cook Vanilla Sauce to a safe temperature (see A Note on Egg Safety, page 26). But with experience you will not even need a thermometer to tell when your sauce is adequately cooked.

1. Whisk the sugar and egg yolks together in a medium bowl.

2. Combine the milk and vanilla beans in a heavy saucepan, and bring to a boil.

3. Slowly dribble ¹/₄ cup of the hot milk into the egg yolk mixture, whisking constantly. Dribble another ¹/₄ cup of the milk into the egg yolk mixture, again whisking constantly.

4. Whisk the egg yolk mixture back into the milk, and return the pan to the heat. Cook over low heat, stirring constantly with a wooden spoon or rubber spatula, until the mixture shows the first sign of coming to a boil. Then quickly strain the sauce into a bowl, and allow it to cool to room temperature. Remove the vanilla beans. Use immediately, or refrigerate in an airtight container for up to 3 days.

VANILLA ICE CREAM

Makes 1 quart

5 large egg yolks

¹/₂ cup plus 2 tablespoons sugar

2 cups whole or 2-percent milk

2 vanilla beans, split

¹/₄ cup heavy cream

Even super-premium brands of ice cream contain gelatins and gums. That's why making your own—with nothing more than cream, milk, eggs, and a vanilla bean—is so rewarding. With today's inexpensive ice cream machines (see Resources, page 283) homemade ice cream is within everybody's reach. Because it contains no preservatives and no thickeners, this ice cream is best eaten as soon as it is churned, or shortly after, although it will keep in an airtight container in the freezer for a day or two.

1. Combine the egg yolks and the sugar in the bowl of an electric mixer fitted with the whisk attachment, and whip until the mixture is pale yellow and has increased in volume, about 2 minutes.

2. Pour the milk into a heavy saucepan. Scrape the seeds from the vanilla beans into the milk and then add the scraped beans to the pan. Slowly bring to a boil over medium heat. Dribble the hot milk, a few tablespoons at a time, into the egg mixture, whisking constantly. Once you have whisked in all of the milk, return the mixture to the saucepan and cook over medium-low heat, stirring constantly with a wooden spoon, until the edges just begin to bubble and the mixture has the consistency of heavy cream.

3. Remove the mixture from the heat and pour it through a fine-mesh strainer into a bowl. Allow it to cool to lukewarm, and then refrigerate until it is completely chilled, 2 to 3 hours.

4. Stir the heavy cream into the custard, and freeze in an ice cream maker according to the manufacturer's instructions.

HONEY VANILLA ICE CREAM

Makes 1 quart

5 large egg yolks

¾ cup honey, preferably clover honey

2 cups whole or 2-percent milk

2 whole vanilla beans

¼ cup heavy cream

This ice cream is sweetened with honey instead of sugar. Use it as you would plain Vanilla Ice Cream. Be aware that ice cream made with honey never gets as hard as ice cream made with sugar.

1. Combine the egg yolks and honey in the bowl of an electric mixer fitted with the whisk attachment, and whip until the mixture is pale yellow and has increased in volume, about 2 minutes.

2. Pour the milk into a heavy saucepan. Scrape the seeds from the vanilla beans into the milk and then add the scraped vanilla beans to the pan. Slowly bring to a boil over medium heat. Dribble the hot milk, a few tablespoons at a time, into the egg mixture, whisking constantly. Once you have whisked in half of the milk, return the mixture to the saucepan and cook over medium-low heat, stirring constantly with a wooden spoon, until the edges just begin to bubble and the mixture has the consistency of heavy cream.

3. Remove the mixture from the heat and pour it through a fine-mesh strainer into a bowl. Allow it to cool to lukewarm, and then refrigerate until it is completely chilled, 2 to 3 hours.

4. Stir the heavy cream into the custard, and freeze in an ice cream maker according to the manufacturer's instructions.

PEANUT BUTTER CREAM

Makes about 5 cups

14 tablespoons (1³/₄ sticks) unsalted butter, softened

1¹/₂ cups smooth peanut butter

¹/₄ cup confectioners' sugar

Pinch salt

3 cups heavy cream, chilled

Use this flavorful buttercream as a cake or roulade filling, instead of whipped cream or plain buttercream. One word of caution: Do not work it too much, or the fat from the peanut butter will separate. Use it as soon as you mix it, and don't spread it around too much, or it will lose its shiny smoothness.

1. Place the butter in the bowl of an electric mixer fitted with the paddle attachment, and beat until light and fluffy. Add the peanut butter, confectioners' sugar, and salt, and beat until smooth and well incorporated, 3 to 4 minutes.

2. Whip the heavy cream in an electric mixer fitted with the whisk attachment until it holds stiff peaks. Fold the whipped cream into the peanut butter mixture, taking care not to deflate the cream.

FRENCH BUTTERCREAM

Makes about 7 cups

5 large eggs

2 cups sugar

¹/₂ cup water

1 tablespoon light corn syrup

2¹/₂ cups (5 sticks) unsalted butter, softened

1 tablespoon pure vanilla extract

Pinch salt

This is a simple buttercream that keeps well—good for when you want to make a cake a day or more in advance. It is easy enough to vary the flavor: For chocolate buttercream, beat in 2 tablespoons unsweetened cocoa powder per cup of buttercream. For lemon, beat in ¹/₂ cup Lemon Cream (page 250) for every cup of buttercream. To flavor buttercream with a liqueur, beat in 1¹/₂ tablespoons rum, Grand Marnier, pear brandy, or raspberry brandy per cup of buttercream.

1. Place the eggs in the bowl of an electric mixer fitted with the whisk attachment.

2. Combine the sugar, water, and corn syrup in a small saucepan and cook until the mixture reaches the soft ball stage (235 degrees on a candy thermometer).

3. Turn the mixer on high speed and pour the syrup into the eggs in a slow, steady stream, making sure that none of it falls on the whisk. Continue to whip on high speed until the mixture is fluffy and has cooled to warm room temperature.

4. Beat in the butter until smooth, about 2 minutes. Stir in the vanilla and salt. The buttercream should be silky, with the consistency of thick mayonnaise. (If the buttercream separates during beating, your ingredients were probably too cold. Place the bowl on top of a pot of barely simmering water to warm it up. Do not overheat; you don't want the butter to begin to melt. Return it to the mixer and beat until smooth.)

5. Use immediately, or cover with plastic wrap and refrigerate for up to 4 days. French Buttercream can be frozen in an airtight container for up to 1 month; defrost it in the refrigerator overnight. Chilled buttercream must be brought to room temperature and rewhipped before using.

AMERICAN BUTTERCREAM

Makes 1½ cups

8 tablespoons (1 stick) unsalted butter, softened

2 tablespoons solid vegetable shortening

1¼ cups confectioners' sugar

2 tablespoons milk, warmed

This very simple buttercream is perfect when you want to embellish a cake with just a few piped decorations and don't want to go to the trouble of making a batch of French Buttercream. But it is also good for wedding cakes and birthday cakes; you can use it in place of rolled fondant because it finishes so beautifully and pipes so well. Color it by adding food coloring, drop by drop, until you achieve the desired color; avoiding over-coloring it. A tip: You can color a portion of it and pipe roses on a parchment-lined baking sheet. Then freeze the sheet, and use a spatula to transfer the frozen buttercream roses to your frosted cake.

1. Combine the butter and shortening in the bowl of an electric mixer fitted with the paddle attachment. Beat on medium-high speed until fluffy, scraping down the sides of the bowl several times as necessary.

2. Add the confectioners' sugar, ½ cup at a time, mixing on low speed after each addition so the sugar doesn't fly out of the bowl.

3. With the mixer running, add the milk. Beat on high speed, scraping down the sides of the bowl once or twice as necessary, until the buttercream is light and fluffy, about 4 minutes.

4. Use immediately, or refrigerate in an airtight container for up to 1 week. Bring to room temperature and rewhip before using.

ENGLISH CUSTARD COFFEE BUTTERCREAM

Makes about 6 cups

2 cups whole milk

2 cups freshly ground coffee beans

8 large egg yolks

2 cups sugar

3 cups (6 sticks) unsalted butter, at room temperature

This is absolutely my best-tasting buttercream, with a lighter and silkier texture than French Buttercream. Infusing the milk with ground coffee gives it a much smoother flavor than instant espresso powder would. I always flavor this rich buttercream with coffee, but if you'd like to experiment with a vanilla version, replace the coffee with a vanilla bean.

1. Combine the milk and the ground coffee in a medium saucepan and bring to a boil. Remove from the heat and allow to steep for 4 minutes. Strain into a large measuring cup. If it falls a little short of 2 cups because of the straining, add a little more milk to make an even 2 cups.

2. Return the milk mixture to the pan and bring to a boil. Whisk the egg yolks and sugar together in a medium bowl. Very slowly dribble 2 tablespoons of the hot milk mixture into the egg yolk mixture, whisking constantly. Dribble another ¼ cup into the egg yolk mixture, again whisking constantly.

3. Whisk the egg yolk mixture back into the milk mixture, and return the pan to the heat. Cook over medium heat, stirring with a wooden spoon or rubber spatula, until the mixture is just about to boil. Strain it into a clean bowl and let it cool to room temperature.

4. Place the butter in the bowl of an electric mixer fitted with the whisk attachment. Whisk the butter until it is light and fluffy. Slowly whisk in the cool custard, and beat until it is light and creamy.

(cont. on next page)

5. Use immediately, or refrigerate in an airtight container for up to 3 days before using. Chilled English Custard Coffee Buttercream must be brought to room temperature and rewhipped before using.

GANACHE

Makes 2 cups

12 ounces bittersweet or semisweet chocolate, chopped, or one 12-ounce bag semisweet chocolate chips

1 cup heavy cream

For the smoothest ganache glaze, don't stir it too much before spreading it, or you will stir air bubbles into it, which will burst when you spread it on a cake. Use it at warm room temperature, and freeze your cake for 30 minutes first in order to chill the surface so the ganache will set up quickly after it is applied. Ganache can also be used between thin layers of cake. I like to slice a Perfect Yellow Cake (page 31) into as many layers as I can and then sandwich them back together with ganache.

Ganache can also be whipped and used to fill cakes, to pipe rosettes onto the tops of cakes, and to pipe decorations onto cupcakes. To whip Ganache, cool it to room temperature and then transfer it to an electric mixer fitted with the whisk attachment. Whip until it is light and fluffy. It should lighten in color and resemble chocolate buttercream.

Place the chocolate in a heatproof bowl. Bring the cream to a near boil in a small saucepan. Pour the hot cream over the chocolate and whisk until smooth. Cool to room temperature. Use immediately, or refrigerate in an airtight container for up to 2 weeks and then warm in a microwave until soft before using.

QUICK CHOCOLATE MOUSSE

Serves 6

4 ounces semisweet or bittersweet chocolate, finely chopped

1 cup heavy cream, at room temperature

1½ teaspoons pure vanilla extract

This mousse is best used as soon as it is made, when it is very soft and spreadable. Use it as a cake filling, or use it as a garnish for a slice of plain cake. There's nothing I like better than a slice of Coffee Genoise warm from the oven, with a scoop of this mousse and maybe a few fresh raspberries on the side.

Handle the ingredients carefully for the best results. The chocolate should be a little warm to the touch; otherwise it may set before you have a chance to fold it into the cream, resulting in a grainy mousse. For the same reason, let the cream come to room temperature before you whip it. If it is too cold, it might cause the chocolate to harden too quickly.

1. Pour 2 inches of water into a medium saucepan and bring to a bare simmer. Place the chocolate in a stainless-steel bowl that is large enough to rest on top of the saucepan, and place it on top of the simmering water, making sure that the bowl doesn't touch the water. Heat, whisking occasionally, until the chocolate is completely melted. Remove the bowl from the heat and let cool slightly until the chocolate is just warm to the touch, between 95 and 100 degrees on an instant-read thermometer.

2. Combine the cream and the vanilla in the bowl of an electric mixer fitted with the whisk attachment and whip until it holds soft peaks. Whisk the whipped cream into the chocolate quickly and all at once.

(cont. on next page)

3. If you are using the mousse as a cake filling, spread it on the cake layers while it is still soft. To serve it as a garnish or by itself, scrape the mousse into a large serving bowl or into individual goblets. Serve it immediately, or refrigerate it in an airtight container for up to 1 day before serving.

SEMISWEET CHOCOLATE GLAZE

Makes about 2 1/2 cups

One 12-ounce bag (2 cups) semisweet chocolate chips

1 cup plus 6 tablespoons heavy cream

This glaze is thinner than ganache because it doesn't contain as much chocolate. Use it when you want to pour a very thin, shiny coat of chocolate over a cake. It is also just the right consistency to be a topping for ice cream.

Place the chocolate in a heatproof bowl. Bring the cream to a near boil in a small saucepan. Pour the hot cream over the chocolate and whisk until smooth. Cool to room temperature. Refrigerate in an airtight container for up to 1 month, and rewarm it to warm room temperature on top of the stove or in the microwave before using.

LIGHT CHOCOLATE SAUCE

Makes 2 cups

8 ounces semisweet chocolate, chopped, or semisweet chocolate chips

1 1/2 cups water

1/4 cup sugar

This chocolate syrup will remain liquid, even when poured over ice cream.

Place the chocolate in a heatproof bowl. Bring the water and sugar to a boil in a small saucepan. Pour the boiling water mixture over the chocolate and whisk until smooth. Use warm, or refrigerate in an airtight container for up to 1 month and then rewarm on top of the stove or in the microwave before using.

LEMON GLAZE

Makes about ½ cup

1 cup confectioners' sugar

2 tablespoons fresh lemon juice

1 teaspoon grated lemon zest

This glaze gives freshly baked cakes a beautiful shine and an appealing crunch.

Whisk the confectioners' sugar, lemon juice, and lemon zest together in a small bowl until smooth. Use immediately, or cover with plastic wrap and refrigerate for up to 1 week.

RASPBERRY SAUCE

Makes 2¼ cups

Two 12-ounce bags frozen unsweetened raspberries, thawed, or 1½ pounds fresh raspberries

½ cup sugar, or more to taste

Frozen raspberries make the best raspberry sauce. Somehow, during freezing the flavor of the fruit intensifies (this is just the opposite with strawberries, which lose much of their flavor during freezing). The sweetness of berries varies, so taste your sauce and add more sugar if it is too tart.

Combine the raspberries and sugar in a blender and blend until smooth. Push through a fine-mesh strainer into a bowl. Use immediately, refrigerate in an airtight container for 2 days, or freeze for up to 3 weeks.

BLUEBERRY SAUCE

Makes 4 cups

3 tablespoons cornstarch

$1/2$ cup water

2 pints blueberries, washed
and stemmed

1 cup sugar

$1/4$ cup fresh lemon juice

This sauce is wonderful over vanilla ice cream, as well as with many cakes. Take care not to crush the blueberries as they cook. You want the liquid to thicken and the fruit to soften but stay intact.

1. Combine the cornstarch and $1/4$ cup of the water in a small bowl. Whisk until smooth. Set aside.

2. Combine the blueberries, the remaining $1/4$ cup water, and the sugar in a small saucepan. Bring to a simmer over medium heat, and cook for 1 minute. Shake the pot occasionally to prevent sticking, but do not stir or you will break up the berries.

3. Pour the mixture into a strainer set over a bowl to separate the berries from the juice. Return the juice to the saucepan. Stir in the lemon juice. Bring to a boil, and stir in the cornstarch mixture. Boil, stirring constantly, until the juice has thickened, 2 to 3 minutes. Remove from the heat and carefully stir in the berries. Use warm; or refrigerate in an airtight container for up to 3 days and then rewarm slowly, without stirring, before using.

ORANGE SAUCE

Makes 1 cup

¹/₂ cup strained apricot jam

2 tablespoons Grand Marnier

2 tablespoons water

1 navel orange, peeled, all pith removed, and cut into small cubes

The fresh juicy oranges give a nice acidity to this sauce, enlivened by Grand Marnier. Use it over plain vanilla ice cream, or spooned over slices of yellow cake with a scoop of vanilla ice cream on the side.

Stir the jam, Grand Marnier, and water together in a medium bowl. Stir in the orange pieces and their juices. Use immediately, or refrigerate in an airtight container for up to 1 week.

CHUNKY STRAWBERRY SAUCE

Makes 1¹/₂ cups

1 pint strawberries, washed, allowed to air-dry, and stemmed

¹/₂ cup confectioners' sugar

1 tablespoon Cointreau or other orange-flavored liqueur

¹/₂ tablespoon fresh lemon juice

Fresh, not frozen, strawberries are a must for this simple sauce. Use it with Blueberry Sauce and Orange Sauce over slices of Perfect Yellow Cake for a simple but very pretty dessert.

Combine the strawberries, confectioners' sugar, Cointreau, and lemon juice in a medium bowl and mash with a potato masher until some of the berries release their juices but you still have a lot of large pieces of berries. Use immediately, or refrigerate in an airtight container for up to 2 days. Do not freeze.

APRICOT SAUCE

About 1½ cups

One 15-ounce can apricot halves in syrup

There is no simpler fruit sauce than this one, made of pureed canned apricots.

Place the apricot halves, with their syrup, in a blender and puree until smooth. Apricot Sauce will keep, refrigerated in an airtight container, for up to 2 weeks.

MANGO SAUCE

Makes 1½ cups

1 large mango, peeled, seeded, and cut into 1-inch chunks

1 tablespoon sugar

1 tablespoon fresh lime juice

Mango, with its wonderful aroma and flavor, always reminds me of far-off, exotic places. It goes well with many cakes in this book, especially the Banana Bundt Cake (page 48).

Combine the mango, sugar, and lime juice in a blender and puree until smooth. Push the puree through a fine-mesh strainer into a bowl. Mango Sauce will keep, refrigerated in an airtight container, for up to 2 days.

LIGHT SYRUP

Makes 1 quart

4 cups water

2 cups sugar

Combine the water and sugar in a medium saucepan and bring to a boil. Remove from the heat and allow to cool to room temperature. Use immediately, or refrigerate in an airtight container for up to 2 weeks.

HEAVY SYRUP

Makes 2 cups

1 cup water

1½ cups sugar

1 tablespoon light corn syrup

Combine the water, sugar, and corn syrup in a small saucepan and bring to a boil. Remove from the heat and allow to cool to room temperature. Use immediately, or refrigerate in an airtight container for up to 1 month.

NOUGAT

Makes about 3 cups, crushed

2 cups sugar

2 cups sliced blanched almonds

This is a very versatile and simple candy. Use shards of it to decorate a cake; or crush it in a food processor or with a rolling pin, and press the crumbles into the sides of a cake or fold them into a filling or frosting. If you'd like, substitute 1½ cups unsalted roasted peanuts for the almonds.

1. Line a rimmed baking sheet with a Silpat. Place the sugar in a heavy saucepan. Cook over medium-high heat, stirring constantly, until the sugar melts and turns a uniform amber color, 5 to 7 minutes. Stir in the sliced almonds, and pour the nougat onto the prepared baking sheet.

2. Immediately place another Silpat on top of the hot nougat and use a rolling pin to roll it out very thin. Let cool completely. Nougat will keep in an airtight container at room temperature for up to 2 weeks.

TUXEDO STRAWBERRIES

Make 18 strawberries

18 large strawberries, stems intact

1 pound tempered white chocolate (page 279)

1 pound tempered dark chocolate (page 279)

These make a beautiful decoration for the First Ladies' Strawberry Cake, but they are also beautiful on their own or as part of a petit four tray. Choose ripe but not soft strawberries; berries that are overripe will ooze some of their liquid and ruin the chocolate coating. If at all possible, keep these at room temperature; they will taste much better than if chilled. But if the weather is very warm, it's best to keep them in the refrigerator.

1. Use a small towel to wipe the strawberries clean. Do not wash them with water, as the moisture will ruin the chocolate. Line a baking sheet with parchment paper.

2. Dip each strawberry into the white chocolate, covering it completely, with the chocolate as close to the stem as possible. Scrape any excess chocolate from the back of the strawberry onto the edge of the bowl. Place the covered strawberries, on the flattest side, on the parchment-lined baking sheet, and let stand until the chocolate is completely set, 5 to 10 minutes.

3. Line another baking sheet with parchment paper. Dip first one side of the strawberries and then the other into the dark chocolate, leaving a V-shape of white chocolate still visible, again scraping the excess dark chocolate from the back onto the side of the bowl. (The dark chocolate is the tuxedo "jacket" and the white chocolate is the "shirt.") Place the berries, scraped side down, on the clean parchment paper. Let stand until the dark chocolate is completely set, 5 to 10 minutes.

4. Place the remaining dark chocolate in a pastry bag fitted with a very small plain tip, or in a paper cornet (see page 281). Pipe a little bow tie on the top part of the white chocolate on each berry. Then pipe a few little dots descending from the bow tie to look like buttons. Let stand until the bow ties and buttons are set.

5. Let stand, lightly draped with plastic wrap, at room temperature for up to 1 day.

PUFF PASTRY

Makes 2½ pounds

FOR THE DOUGH:

1½ teaspoons salt

1½ cups water

3¼ cups all-purpose flour

3 tablespoons unsalted butter

FOR THE BUTTER LAYER:

¾ cup all-purpose flour, plus more for sprinkling

2 cups (4 sticks) unsalted butter, chilled

Homemade puff pastry is challenging but also exciting. Whenever I bake a batch, I can't wait to see how high I can get it to rise, trying to top myself every time. Puff pastry can be put to so many uses—tarts, turnovers, napoleons, savory hors d'oeuvres, wrapping fish or beef, or maybe just as a fleuron to be served with a meal.

Make sure your puff pastry is completely baked; otherwise the center will look and taste like cardboard. I like to prop the oven door open slightly with the handle of a wooden spoon or a small ball of aluminum foil. This releases any moisture from the oven and allows the pastry to really dry out during the last part of baking.

1. For the dough: Place the salt and ¼ cup of the water in the bowl of an electric mixer fitted with the paddle attachment, and stir to dissolve the salt. Add the flour and the butter, and mix on low speed until the butter is completely mixed in and no pieces are visible. Add 1 cup of the water and continue to mix until the dough comes together; it should be very firm but not hard. If it won't come together or is too hard, add some of the remaining ¼ cup water, 1 tablespoon at a time, until the dough has the consistency of pie dough.

2. Turn the dough out onto a lightly floured work surface and roll it into a ball. With a sharp paring knife, make a ¼-inch-deep cut across the top of the dough ball to release its elasticity. Place the dough on a baking sheet, cover with plastic wrap, and let it rest in the refrigerator for 2 hours.

3. For the butter layer: Sprinkle 2 or 3 tablespoons of flour on a work surface, and place the chilled sticks of butter on the flour. Sprinkle the ¾ cup flour over the butter. Pound the butter with a rolling pin until it comes together in one mass, turning it over often and sprinkling it with more flour as necessary so that the butter does not stick to the work surface or to the rolling pin. Continue to pound and turn until the butter is a soft and pliable doughy square measuring about 6 x 6 inches, with no cracks or crumbling around the edge. If the butter begins to get sticky or begins to melt, place it in the refrigerator until chilled and then begin to work it again. Place the floured butter on a plate and refrigerate it for 30 minutes.

4. Scrape the work surface with a dough scraper to remove any remaining butter. Lightly flour the surface and roll the puff pastry dough into a 10-inch square. Place the pounded butter in the center of the square, arranging it so that each corner of the butter square is pointing to the middle of each side of the dough. Fold the corners of the dough over until they meet in the center of the butter square, enclosing the butter.

(cont. on next page)

5. Sprinkle the folded dough with a little flour, and roll it over to form a rectangle measuring about 10 x 22 inches. With one short side facing you, fold the bottom third of the dough over the middle third, and then fold the top third of the dough over these two layers, as if you were folding a letter to be placed in an envelope. This is called a single turn—it creates three layers of dough. Put the dough back on the baking sheet, cover it with plastic wrap, and refrigerate for 30 minutes to rest and firm up.

6. Flour the work surface again, and remove the puff pastry dough from the refrigerator. Place it on the work surface with a short side facing you. Roll it out again into a 10 x 22-inch rectangle. Fold the top edge down so that it comes to the middle of the dough. Fold the bottom edge up so that it meets the top edge in the middle of the dough. Fold the dough in half again, from top to bottom. This is called a double turn—it creates four layers of dough. Return the dough to the baking sheet, cover it, and refrigerate it for another 30 minutes.

7. Repeat Step 5, rolling the dough out and giving it a single turn. Refrigerate it for 30 minutes to 1 hour.

8. Repeat Step 6, rolling the dough out and giving it a double turn.

9. Wrap the dough in plastic wrap and let it rest in the refrigerator for 2 to 3 hours before using. Or wrap it in plastic and then in foil and freeze it for up to 2 months. Defrost it in the refrigerator overnight before using.

DECORATING BASICS

A simply decorated cake is much more appealing than an overdone one. I'd rather see a cake edged with a perfect row of buttercream rosettes than one covered with a tangle of flowers, leaves, and vines. I prefer one exquisite and unique marzipan rose on top to a profusion of identical flowers made without care. Not only that, but I'd rather eat a simply decorated cake! Too many embellishments will overwhelm the flavor of the cake underneath.

Most of the recipes in this book contain specific instructions for decorating them, but you should feel free to experiment. There are decorating techniques that I use over and over, and I've gathered them together here for your convenience. You will find instructions for piping whipped cream, buttercream, and whipped ganache into simple patterns; making simple marzipan flowers and figures; using chocolate to make curls, write messages, and draw on cakes; and tempering chocolate for items like Tuxedo Strawberries (page 266), where a shiny finish is crucial. Whichever technique you choose, take extreme care with a modest decoration, and your cake will be beautiful. I guarantee it.

The following list is brief. I chose these particular techniques for their versatility and ease. Anyone can achieve any of the effects with patience and a little practice. For instructions on making sugar decorations, which can be beautiful but are more challenging and trickier than anything here, see my earlier book, *Dessert University*.

Piping Whipped Cream, Buttercream, and Whipped Ganache

Use a disposable plastic pastry bag, or a reusable canvas pastry bag, fitted with an appropriate tip to pipe simple cake decorations with buttercream, whipped ganache, or whipped cream. Smaller plain and star tips make the most delicate buttercream and ganache decorations. When piping whipped cream, use large tips, as smaller ones will deflate the cream. To fill a pastry bag and begin piping, follow these steps:

1. If you are using a disposable bag, snip off enough of the end so that the bottom half of the tip will fit snugly in the hole and not slide through. Place the desired tip in the bag and fill the bag no more than halfway to the top with your frosting. If you fill it any higher than this, you will have trouble twisting it closed and the frosting will ooze out the top as you work.

2. Push the frosting toward the bottom of the bag by holding the top of the bag closed with one hand and sliding the fingers of your other hand down the sides of the bag toward the bottom. Once all of the frosting is in the bottom of the bag, twist the top tightly to seal it.

3. Hold the bag in your right hand (or in your left, if you are left-handed), grasping it with your thumb and forefinger at the point where it has been twisted. Use your other three fingers to squeeze the dough from the bag. Use your left hand to steady the bottom of the bag as you move it over the cake.

TO MAKE STARS Use a star tip. Hold the bag at a 90-degree angle about ¼ inch from the surface of the cake. Squeeze out a star shape, stop squeezing, and then lift the tip from the frosting. (If you lift the tip while still piping, you'll create an unwanted peak of frosting.) For a star border, pipe stars close together so there are no spaces between them, piping them as uniformly as possible.

TO MAKE ROSETTES Use a star tip. Hold the bag at a 90-degree angle about ¼ inch from the surface of the cake. Squeeze and at the same time move your right hand to the left and up and around in a circular motion, coming back to the starting point. Stop squeezing and then pull the tip away from the rosette. Make a rosette border by piping rosettes close together, all around the edge of the cake.

TO MAKE A SHELL BORDER Use a star tip. Hold the bag at a 45-degree angle with the tip ¼ inch from the surface of the cake. Squeeze the bag with a good amount of pressure, so that the frosting comes out in a wide fan shape. Gradually decrease the pressure on the bag as you lower the tip to the surface of the cake. Stop squeezing, and lift the tip from the frosting. Start piping another shell right on top of the skinny tip of the last one, so that the wide end of the new shell covers the tip of the previous one. Continue all around the bottom edge of the cake until you have reached your starting point.

TO MAKE A LATTICE PATTERN Use a large plain or star tip. Holding the bag at a 90-degree angle, pipe a border for your lattice along the outer edge of the cake. Then, starting at about 10 o'clock on the cake, pipe a diagonal string from 10 to 4 o'clock, attaching each end to the outline. On either side of the first string, pipe parallel diagonal strings, about ½ inch apart. Next, starting at about 2 o'clock on the cake, pipe a diagonal string from 2 to 8 o'clock, attaching each end to the outline. Pipe strings parallel to this one, as before, to form the lattice.

Marzipan Decorations

Marzipan is relatively easy to work with and can be molded into an infinite number of flowers and decorative figures. In my opinion, it is one of the most satisfying ways to add beauty to a cake.

Marzipan is available from pastry suppliers in larger quantities than you will be able to find at the supermarket (see Resources, page 283). I have found mail-order marzipan to be fresher than the kind sold at the supermarket. Marzipan is highly sensitive to the air and if it sits on the shelf too long and is not stored properly, it will dry out and become crusty and granular, making it impossible to mold.

Marzipan should be pliable but stiff enough to hold its shape. If yours is too soft when you unwrap it, knead a little confectioners' sugar into it to stiffen it up. If it is too hard, soften it by adding a little Heavy Syrup (page 265), drop by drop, until it is workable. In any case, knead it for a few seconds before you begin to warm it up. But don't overknead it—this will release the almond oil and ruin it for molding. To color the marzipan before molding it, just knead a little food coloring into it, again taking care not to overknead. As you work, keep any marzipan that you are not using covered with plastic wrap, or it will dry out and form a crust. Wrap leftover marzipan tightly in plastic wrap and store it at room temperature. It will keep for up to 1 month—any longer than this and it will begin to lose its freshness and pliability.

If you are decorating a cake with marzipan, you need to plan ahead so that your decorations will be hard enough to handle. Small flowers will harden up in about 1 day, and larger figures will take 2 days to harden. Once hard, they will keep in an airtight container for up to 1 week.

Marzipan Leaves and Ladybugs

Little ladybugs on green leaves adorn the Brioche "Peaches" (page 44). You can also use these pretty decorations on top of any summertime cake.

1. For the leaves: Line a baking sheet with parchment paper, and set it aside. Color a little ball of marzipan with green food coloring. Lightly dust a work surface with confectioners' sugar and roll out the marzipan so it is very thin, using an offset spatula to lift it from the counter as you roll so it won't stick.

2. Cut small leaf shapes, no bigger than 1 inch long, with a sharp paring knife. Use the dull side of the knife to make indentations on the leaves to resemble veins. Place the leaves on the prepared baking sheet.

3. For the stems, roll the remaining green marzipan into a thin tube about the diameter of a pencil. Cut the tube into 1-inch lengths. On one end, make an indentation. This will be the end that sticks out from the peach. Place them on the prepared baking sheet.

4. To form the ladybugs: Color a small ball of marzipan with red food coloring. Take a very small piece of the red marzipan, the size of the tiniest green pea, and roll it into a ball. Lightly press the ball onto the parchment-lined baking sheet to flatten the bottom. Use the side of a toothpick to make an indentation down the center of the ball. Repeat with as many balls as you need.

5. Dip the toothpick in a little melted chocolate and make chocolate spots on either side of the indentation on each ladybug. Use the same toothpick to dab a larger spot of chocolate at one end of the indentation to make the head. Let the ladybugs stand on the parchment-lined baking sheet, along with the leaves and stems, until hardened, about 1 day.

6. Dab the ends of the stems with light corn syrup and stick them onto the peaches. Dab the backs of the leaves with corn syrup and stick them onto the peaches. Put a tiny amount of jam or corn syrup on the underside of each ladybug, and stick it on a leaf.

Marzipan Santas

I like to place a few marzipan Santas around my Bûche de Noël, along with meringue mushrooms. They're simple to make, and they delight the children.

1. Roll a piece of uncolored marzipan into a ball about the size of a small lime. Lightly press one end of it onto a work surface to flatten the bottom. This will be Santa's body.

2. Roll two smaller pieces of red marzipan into log shapes about 2½ inches long and ½ inch thick. Each one will be an arm. Lightly brush the back of each log with beaten egg white, and arrange each arm so that it reaches from Santa's back, down the side of the body, and across his belly.

3. Roll a small piece of uncolored marzipan into a ball about the size of a large marble, and fix it to the top of the body with a little egg white.

4. Roll a piece of white marzipan into a flat V shape for Santa's beard. Use small scissors to snip the edges to make it look like fringe. Fix the beard to the head with egg white.

5. Make two indentations in the head for the eyes. Fill in the indentations with melted chocolate or blue icing. Fix a tiny red ball in the center of the head for a nose, and another one right below it for a mouth.

6. Roll a small piece of red icing into a cone shape to make a cap. Top the cap with a little ball of white marzipan. Glue the cap to the head with egg white. Let the Santa stand, uncovered, at room temperature until completely dried, about 2 days.

Marzipan Roses

Marzipan roses are not difficult to make, and they instantly add beauty to any cake. Color your marzipan with any color that occurs in nature (yellow, pink, red, peach— but no blue roses, please!) Place a leaf or two (page 275) under each one if desired. I suggest eight petals per rose, but you may attach a few or as many as you like.

1. Color the marzipan as desired and adjust its consistency so it is firm enough that the petals won't droop. Roll eight pieces of marzipan into balls about the size of large marbles. Roll another piece into a ball that is about three times the size of one of these marbles.

2. Form the larger ball into a cone. This will be the center of your rose.

3. Spread a small piece of plastic wrap on your work surface. Drape seven of the balls with another piece of plastic wrap to keep them soft. Place the remaining ball on the small piece of plastic wrap and fold the plastic over so it covers the ball. Rub your thumb in a circular motion over the ball to flatten it into a petal shape. Continue to rub one edge until it is paper-thin, leaving the opposite edge thicker. The petal should increase in thickness evenly from top to bottom. The thick edge will form the stable bottom of the petal.

4. Attach the petal to the cone, pressing the thick edge into the bottom of the cone. Repeat with the remaining balls of marzipan, slightly overlapping them on the cone. When you have gone all the way around the cone once, begin with a new layer of petals. The inner petals should be relatively tight and closed, the outer petals more open to resemble a blooming rose. When you have attached all of the petals, pinch the base of the rose and cut off the excess marzipan with a sharp paring knife, so that the rose has a flat bottom to rest on. Place the finished rose on a cardboard cake round or a parchment-lined baking sheet to dry.

Chocolate Shavings and Curls

There is nothing more appetizing than a cake covered with chocolate shavings and curls, and nothing easier. For the best shavings and curls, use dark, milk, or white chocolate that is at warm room temperature. If it isn't warm in your kitchen, set the block under a light for a few minutes (I use the lights under my cabinets for this purpose) to warm it up.

For shavings, use a vegetable peeler to peel away thin strips, letting them fall right into an airtight container. Use immediately or refrigerate the container for up to 1 week before pressing the shavings into the sides of your cake.

For larger curls, hold the block of chocolate with one hand, and with the other hand scrape the edge of a biscuit cutter across the surface. Carefully transfer the curls to an airtight container, and refrigerate them for up to 1 week before showering the top of your cake with them.

Decorating the Sides of a Cake

In the best of all possible worlds, there is no need to decorate the sides of a cake. Either the perfect layers of cake and filling form their own pretty pattern, or a perfectly applied layer of whipped cream or buttercream makes a smooth and simple finish.

But sometimes imperfections in the layering or unevenness in the frosting demand that the sides be covered to create the illusion of perfection. When you need a cake covering, choose from the following list the item that will harmonize with the flavors and textures of the cake: toasted sliced almonds, crushed nougat (page 265), crushed toasted phyllo dough (page 141), cookie crumbs, chocolate shavings.

Press the coating lightly into the sides of a frosted cake, or brush the sides of the cake lightly with strained apricot jam and then press the coating lightly onto the sticky surface.

TEMPERED CHOCOLATE

Makes 1 pound

1 pound bittersweet, dark, milk, or white chocolate, coarsely chopped

To mold chocolate into shiny decorations, such as the "jackets" for the Tuxedo Strawberries (page 266), it is necessary to temper it. Tempering is the process by which chocolate is carefully heated and then cooled and then reheated to ensure that the fat crystals in the cocoa butter don't separate from the cocoa solids and form an unsightly gray "bloom" as the chocolate hardens.

To make sure that the fat crystals in your melted chocolate behave, you have to bring the chocolate to a temperature of 105 degrees, cool it to a temperature of 75 to 80 degrees, and then reheat it to a temperature of about 88 degrees (85 or 86 degrees for milk or white chocolate), but no hotter than this, so that the chocolate is fluid enough to work with but in no danger of going out of temper. To test whether or not your chocolate is in temper, dip the end of a knife into the melted chocolate. It should set up hard and shiny within a minute.

If you are working on a large project and taking a long time, your chocolate will cool in the bowl, becoming too thick to work with. In this case, you will have to rewarm it over a pot of barely simmering water. Take care not to overheat the chocolate, or you will have to start the tempering process all over again. A few seconds over the pot, whisking constantly, should do the trick.

The minimum amount of chocolate that you can temper easily is 1 pound. Smaller quantities are problematic, because as soon as a smaller amount of chocolate is tempered, it will start to harden in the bowl. If you need just a little tempered chocolate, still temper 1 pound. Then let the leftover chocolate solidify, wrap it in plastic, and use it, along with fresh chocolate, the next time you temper a batch.

1. Pour 2 inches of water into a medium-size saucepan and bring to a bare simmer. Place the chocolate in a stainless-steel bowl that is large enough to rest on top of the saucepan, and place it on top of the simmering water, making sure that the bowl doesn't touch the water. Heat, whisking occasionally, until the chocolate is completely melted. Remove the bowl from the heat (leave the saucepan on the stove) and let the chocolate cool slightly until it is just warmer than body temperature, about 100 degrees.

2. Place the bowl on top of a larger bowl of ice water and mix constantly just until the chocolate turns into a paste (75 to 80 degrees), less than 1 minute.

3. Return the bowl to the barely simmering water very briefly, stirring constantly until it is just warm enough to work with again, and no warmer than 88 degrees.

4. To make sure the chocolate is properly tempered, test it before you begin to use it: Place a small amount of chocolate on the tip of a knife. It should set evenly within 1 minute. As you work, make sure to stir the chocolate frequently so that its temperature is even and the chocolate doesn't begin to separate. If it starts to get too thick to work with, place the bowl on top of the barely simmering water very briefly, and stir constantly until it is just warm enough to work with again, and no warmer than 88 degrees. Move the bowl back and forth between the counter and the pot to maintain the right temperature and consistency.

Finely Piped Chocolate Decorations

Melted chocolate can be piped through a cornet, a small cone made of parchment, to make fine lines or writing. It is not necessary to temper the chocolate before piping. Add a few drops of warm water to the hot chocolate (2 drops of water for about 4 tablespoons melted chocolate should be about right). This will thicken it, so it will run less quickly from the cornet, making it easier to work with. To make sure your chocolate is completely lump-free and smooth, pour it through a fine-mesh strainer before pouring it into the cone. Even tiny lumps will clog the opening of the cornet and prevent you from piping smoothly and evenly.

To make and fill a cornet:

1. Cut out a triangle of parchment paper with one side measuring 12 inches and the other two sides measuring 7 inches.

2. Place the triangle on the counter with the long side facing away from you. Bring the far right point down to meet the middle point, curling it under as you bring it down to form a cone shape.

3. Hold the two points tightly together with the thumb and index finger of your right hand. With your left hand, bring the far left point up and around as you did the far right point. All three points should meet at the wide opening of the cone. At the point where the points meet, fold the paper in toward the inside of the cone in ¼-inch pleats to secure the cornet.

4. Close the bottom (the tip) of the cone tightly by sliding the right and left points in opposite directions, away from each other, until the bottom is completely closed. Fill the cone no more than halfway with warm melted chocolate. Roll the top of the cone toward the bottom to seal it, and push the chocolate toward the tip.

5. Cut a pinhole-size opening in the tip, using sharp scissors (if you are using the cone for buttercream or ganache, you'll have to cut a larger opening). Test by writing on a piece of parchment. If the chocolate does not flow freely enough, enlarge the hole slightly and test again.

Writing and Drawing with Chocolate

Use a cornet filled with chocolate to write messages directly onto the surface of a cake: Hold the cornet at a 45-degree angle, with the tip touching the surface of the cake. Drag the cone over the cake as you would a pencil, applying even pressure to the cone to squeeze out the chocolate and forming the letters as you go.

If you do not trust yourself to pipe neatly, there is an alternative: Pipe your writing or decorations onto a sheet of clear plastic (available at stationery stores) set on a baking sheet, holding the cone at a 90-degree angle about 1 inch above the surface of the plastic. Let the chocolate drop onto the plastic as you move the cornet, shaping your letters. If you make a mistake, begin again. Transfer the baking sheet to the refrigerator and chill the chocolate until it is hardened, about 10 minutes. Then slide a small offset spatula underneath the writing and transfer it to the cake.

Chocolate Bicyclists

Use a cornet to draw the chocolate bicyclists that decorate Lance Armstrong's Paris Brest (page 225). Create the shirt by using melted yellow chocolate, available in many craft stores and by mail (see Resources, page 283). Or use a little oil-based yellow food coloring to color the white chocolate.

1. Arrange a piece of parchment paper on a work surface. Fill a paper cornet halfway with tempered chocolate. Cut an opening a little larger than one you would use for writing, about the size of the tip of a ballpoint pen, in the tip of the cornet.

2. Pipe two wheels, each the size of a nickel, onto the parchment, placing them about 1 inch apart. Pipe lines of chocolate to connect the wheels. Pipe the outline of the bicyclist. (See photo insert.) Let set completely.

3. Use the cornet to fill in the bicyclist's shirt with yellow chocolate. Let it set completely before lifting it off the parchment and placing it alongside the cake.

RESOURCES

Most of the cakes in this book can be assembled from ingredients available at the supermarket, using equipment that you already have if you have baked a cake before. For more difficult-to-find items, and for brands I recommend that may not be available in your area, look to the following suppliers:

Candy Direct, Inc.
745 Design Court, Ste. 602
Chula Vista, CA 91911
619-216-0116
www.candydirect.com

Go to this Web site for bulk quantities of Jordan almonds for the Wedding Croquembouche and for French peanuts for Lance Armstrong's Paris Brest.

The Frenchy Bee
866-379-9975
www.thefrenchybee.com

Find Clement Faugier chestnut products here, as well as marzipan and honey imported from France.

King Arthur Flour Company
P.O. Box 876
Norwich, VT 05055-0876
800-827-6836
www.bakerscatalogue.com

You can find almost everything you need to bake a cake in the Baker's Catalogue. The large and reasonably priced selection of equipment includes KitchenAid mixers, baking pans, pastry bags and tips, Silpats, parchment paper, silicone pastry brushes, and candy and instant-read thermometers. Ingredients that your supermarket may not stock, including hazelnut flour, hazelnut praline paste, high-quality vanilla beans, and crystallized ginger, are here too. The Baker's Catalogue also sells an impressive selection of chocolate and cocoa, including five kinds of cocoa powder and several different kinds of dark chocolate, including Scharffen Berger, Merckens, and my favorite, Valhrona. For cake decorating, buy food coloring, coarse sanding sugar, and marzipan here.

Market Hall Foods
5655 College Avenue
Oakland, CA 94618
888-952-4005
www.markethallfoods.com

This online specialty foods purveyor sells a wonderful array of candied fruits and flowers, including rose and violet petals, candied orange peel, candied lemon peel, and crystallized ginger. Also find the entire line of Callebaut baking chocolate, vanilla beans at an excellent price, beautiful hazelnuts imported from Italy, and a great selection of artisanal honeys.

Sur La Table
Pike Place Market
84 Pine Street
Seattle, WA 98101
(and other locations throughout the country)
800-243-0852
www.surlatable.com

This fine cookware shop sells ice cream machines ranging from the Cuisinart Classic Ice Cream Machine (about $50) to the Italian-made Lussino (about $700) as well as KitchenAid mixers in every size and color. In addition to small appliances, it carries hard-to-find kitchen equipment like Silpats, professional melon ballers, channel peelers, and an array of porcelain bakeware including coeur à la crème molds.

Wilton Industries
2240 West 75th Street
Woodridge, IL 60517-0750
800-994-5866
www.wilton.com

In addition to selling cake supplies such as pastry bags and tips, cardboard cake rounds, sanding sugars, and food coloring, Wilton's Web site provides detailed instructions for using a pastry bag and tips to decorate cakes.

EQUIVALENCY TABLES

COMMON MEASUREMENTS

VOLUME TO VOLUME

3 tsp = 1 tbsp

4 tbsp = $\frac{1}{4}$ cup

5$\frac{1}{3}$ tbsp = $\frac{1}{3}$ cup

4 ounces = $\frac{1}{2}$ cup

8 ounces = 1 cup

1 cup = $\frac{1}{2}$ pint

VOLUME TO WEIGHT

$\frac{1}{4}$ cup liquid or fat = 2 ounces

$\frac{1}{2}$ cup liquid or fat = 4 ounces

1 cup liquid or fat = 8 ounces

2 cups liquid or fat = 1 pound

1 cup sugar = 7 ounces

1 cup flour = 5 ounces

METRIC EQUIVALENCIES

LIQUID AND DRY MEASURE EQUIVALENCIES

CUSTOMARY	METRIC
$\frac{1}{4}$ teaspoon	1.25 milliliters
$\frac{1}{2}$ teaspoon	2.5 milliliters
1 teaspoon	5 milliliters
1 tablespoon	15 milliliters
1 fluid ounce	30 milliliters
$\frac{1}{4}$ cup	60 milliliters
$\frac{1}{3}$ cup	80 milliliters
$\frac{1}{2}$ cup	120 milliliters
1 cup	240 milliliters
1 pint (2 cups)	480 milliliters
1 quart (4 cups)	960 milliliters (.96 liter)
1 gallon (4 quarts)	3.84 liters
1 ounce (by weight)	28 grams
$\frac{1}{4}$ pound (4 ounces)	114 grams
1 pound (16 ounces)	454 grams
2.2 pounds	1 kilogram (1000 grams)

OVEN-TEMPERATURE EQUIVALENCIES

DESCRIPTION	°FAHRENHEIT	°CELSIUS
Cool	200	90
Very slow	250	120
Slow	300–325	150–160
Moderately slow	325–350	160–180
Moderate	350–375	180–190
Moderately hot	375–400	190–200
Hot	400–450	200–230
Very hot	450–500	230–260

INDEX

----

288   INDEX